Praise for Kathy Kristof's
Investing 101

"*Investing 101* by Kathy Kristof is a reader-friendly intro-
duction to the basics of investing and personal finance.... **If I
had to suggest a book on investing and personal finance to an
absolute beginner, it would be** *Investing 101.*"
> *BookPage*

"... [an] excellent primer about investing. **Investors will get
a clearer idea of how markets work** and what you can realis-
tically expect from your retirement funds."
> *The Boston Globe*

"Kristof's down-to-earth style and clear prose gives her writing a decidedly user-friendly quality.... **The vast majority of us
worker drones who haven't yet made complete sense of things**
will find *Investing 101* an easy way to get started."
> *Miami Herald*

"In *Investing 101,* Kathy Kristof skillfully guides the novice
investor, step by step, along the path to investment success.
It's **an ideal primer** for anyone who wants to enter the financial world and would like a helping hand."
> MYRON KANDEL
> Financial Editor, CNN

"Not only is this book more simple and straightforward than the typical book on investing, it's also more humorous and personal."
Today's Librarian

"Too many of us give too little thought to the underpinnings of investing: how much risk to shoulder, when to sell, etc. Kathy Kristof explains these basics in language we all can understand. Investing 101 is sure to become a great reference guide for novices and long-time investors alike."
STEVE DINNEN
Personal Finance Columnist
The Des Moines Register

"Kathy Kristof knows investing inside and out. She can take even the most complicated information and make it easy to understand—and entertaining."
ILYCE R. GLINK
National Syndicated Columnist
Author of 100 Questions You Should Ask
about Your Personal Finances

"If you're just getting started in the investing world, this is the book you need. Kathy Kristof's smart, sensible advice demystifies the markets and shows you exactly what you need to know to achieve your financial goals. Investing 101 offers a road map to financial success without gimmicks or secret formulas—and it's a whole lot of fun to read, besides."
LIZ PULLIAM WESTON
Personal Finance Columnist
Los Angeles Times

Investing 101

BLOOMBERG PERSONAL BOOKSHELF

Investing 101

Kathy Kristof

BLOOMBERG PRESS

PRINCETON

Books are available for bulk purchases at special discounts. Special editions or book excerpts can also be created to specifications. For information, please write: Special Markets Department, Bloomberg Press.

This publication contains the author's opinions and is designed to provide accurate and authoritative information. It is sold with the understanding that the author, publisher, and Bloomberg L.P. are not engaged in rendering legal, accounting, investment-planning, or other professional advice. The reader should seek the services of a qualified professional for such advice; the author, publisher, and Bloomberg L.P. cannot be held responsible for any loss incurred as a result of specific investments or planning decisions made by the reader.

First edition published 2000

3 5 7 9 10 8 6 4

Library of Congress Cataloging-in-Publication Data

Kristof, Kathy
    Investing 101 / Kathy Kristof.
      p. cm. --- (Bloomberg personal bookshelf)
    Includes index.
    ISBN 1-57660-044-0 (alk. paper)
    1. Investments. 2. Stocks. 3. Mutual funds. 4. Bonds. 5. Finance, Personal.
  I. Title. II. Series.

    HG4521 .K738 2000
    332.6—dc21   00-039822

Acquired and edited by Kathleen Peterson

Book design by Barbara Diez Goldenberg

To my mom and dad

GLOSSARY 201
Definitions for commonly used jargon so you can
interpret Wall Street speak.

INDEX 207

▬▬▬

LIST OF WORKSHEETS

Acknowledgments

I NEVER PLANNED TO WRITE A BOOK ABOUT INVESTING. I really didn't think I could be that dull. But, my editor at the *Los Angeles Times,* Bill Sing, insisted that consumers were in desperate need of solid advice on how to pick individual stocks; how to diversify their assets; when they should invest in bonds; and how they could get started. They needed this information, and they needed it in a form that actually wouldn't be dull, he argued. Informative, interesting, and short. Just the facts. No jargon. It was a tall order, but he's the boss.

So I wrote a series of investing tutorials—then another series—then another. After responding to hundreds of requests for hard copies, we've added yet more information and made it all into this book. In the process, I learned that Bill was right—again. (I hate that.) Yet, again, I'm indebted. Thanks, Billy.

It's often said that a reporter is only as good as his or her sources. I'm grateful to mine. There are literally hundreds of experts—analysts and money managers from the likes of Merrill Lynch, Oppenheimer & Co., Neuberger & Berman, Fidelity Investments, Vanguard, T. Rowe Price, and others—not to mention literally dozens of brilliant and highly paid tax accountants and financial planners who spent hours chatting about markets, economics, trading strategies, and asset allocation. Some of them are quoted in the following pages; some aren't. Their wisdom contributed greatly to the creation of *Investing 101.*

Much more difficult to thank are my friends and family, who contribute to everything I do in ways both obvious and subtle. With their help and support, it seems as if anything is possible. For you, I am truly blessed. Thank you.

Investing 101

Introduction

B EFORE WE GET STARTED with the serious financial stuff, I'd like to share one of my favorite
stories about investing. It's true, and it illustrates a point
that you need to remember while you're reading this
book—particularly if you're a little nervous about your
ability to invest wisely.

The story starts one dark October day on Wall Street,
when the so-called Asian Currency Crisis struck. The
Dow Jones Industrial Average—a key indicator of market
health—plunged more than 300 points. I, like every other

financial reporter on the planet, was charged with making some sense of it all for the readers of a general-circulation newspaper.

Luckily for me, I work for the *Los Angeles Times,* where dozens of skilled reporters mobilize whenever there's a major news event. As a result, I didn't need to do the straight story—the story replete with numbers and specific details of which stocks fell the most and why. Instead, I was charged with figuring out whether individual investors were in a panic (as the professional investors assumed they would be). Given the fast-paced trading and the rapid decline in stock prices, it was clear that somebody was panicking.

First I called the professional investors. I could almost hear the beads of sweat forming under their starched white collars and gray pinstriped suits. They didn't talk. They sputtered, blurting out incomplete sentences such as: "The Asian financial crisis . . . spreading . . . could create global crisis. Market meltdown. . . . It may be time to sell." Yes, this could be called panic.

Then I called dozens of individual investors. A few were home. A few were at work. Some were at the baseball game. They were not breathless. They were not sweating. (Well, in the interest of accuracy, I don't know for sure about the sweating thing. It's sometimes hot in Los Angeles, even in October. But they didn't sound as if they were sweating.)

Were any of them frantically calling their brokers, trying to sell? Not a one. Instead, the individual investors said what the professionals should have said: Markets go up; markets go down. As long as your investments are appropriate for your goals, you don't need to sweat the day-to-day movements. You can go about your business. Take in the baseball game. Relax.

The next day, the wisdom of the guy and girl on the street won out. Stocks climbed right back. Within a few days, they were higher than they'd been before the onset of the "crisis."

What did the professionals have to say about the currency crisis that had them screaming, "Sell, sell, SELL" the day before? "Ahem. It's better."

The moral of this story: You can invest every bit as wisely as—

and sometimes more wisely than—a professional. Why? The professionals were in a panic for one very good reason: If you manage money for a mutual fund, your gains or losses show up in the newspaper the next day. Mess up, and all the world quickly can see what a dope you are. That's embarrassing. Besides, your pay as a money manager is probably going to be tied to how well your portfolio performed over the course of the year relative either to the market as a whole or to the portfolios managed by a group of your peers. No professional wants to be the last numskull to sell out of a money-losing stock.

You, on the other hand, can be a numskull and only your spouse will know. (This might be the time to point out that "or for poorer" clause in your marital vows.) That gives you time to think. Time to consider whether an investment was a mistake or a wise move that simply needs more time to pan out.

In reality, few people make brilliant choices in the heat of the moment. The smartest thing to do when faced with a "catastrophe"—or a "hot stock"—is to take a deep breath and think for a moment.

What should you think about? That's precisely what the rest of this book is all about. It will help you determine how different types of investments react in different markets—and how to choose specific investments in good times and bad. It will even explain when you ought to invest on your own and when you ought to consider hiring a professional to help. With that knowledge, you can weather any investment storm.

Better yet, you can do it calmly, rationally, and with an eye to what matters in life, which, incidentally, is not the size of your portfolio.

So, read. Learn. Enjoy. And then do me one favor: Vow to spend more time with your family and friends than you spend with your portfolio. I guarantee you, it's not going to matter if you have $10 million when you die if you have no one you care about to leave it to.

chapter 1

Exorcising Your Demons

THIS BOOK IS going to tell you how to invest wisely. It's simple. It's straightforward. You'll get step-by-step instructions. Anyone who reads and follows the directions will find it's easy to do.

But following even the most logical instructions may be difficult if, like many people, you've developed a bad habit or two over time. In fact, we all have our demons—our little psychological hurdles that stop us from doing the things that we know to be logical, reasonable, and smart.

Some of these hurdles are caused by our upbringing or culture; some seem to strike men and not women—or women and not men. But no matter the cause, we need to get over them if we're to have any hope of investing wisely enough to have more money than regrets in our old age.

I'm not a psychologist, so you shouldn't expect that buying this book is going to save you from a lifetime of therapy expenses. In fact, I don't know what particular complex or syndrome or short-coming affects you. But following the adage that "recognizing the problem is the first step to fixing it," I can tell you some problems that I've seen frequently over the years and whom they usually seem to strike, as well as a few simple moves you can make to overcome each obstacle.

Women

B Y AND LARGE, WOMEN START INVESTING LATER IN LIFE THAN MEN, SET LESS MONEY ASIDE, AND INVEST MORE conservatively. That has the unpleasant effect of leaving them poor in their old age. Some 80 percent of the elderly people living in poverty are women. So what's their excuse?

❏   **The poor girl:** "I would invest, but I just don't have the money," says the perfectly coiffed twenty-five-year-old as she slams the door of her BMW in the mall parking lot. "I'm going to start just as soon as I get a raise."

OK. That was a slight exaggeration. And we all know that women do earn less, on average, than men. It would be easier to save if you earned more money. But sometimes life is just not fair. Get over it.

Now, be fair with yourself and answer honestly: When was the last time you bought lunch or dinner at a restaurant instead of going for the cheaper alternative of packing a sack lunch or making your own dinner? When was the last time you bought a suit, sweater, skirt, or pair of shoes that you knew you didn't need? (And if you said "Never," just how exactly did you define the word *need*? Did you need it because you wanted it really, really bad? Or because it was on sale and you might need it before it was next on sale?)

If you have a job that pays a decent wage—that's anything that keeps you above the poverty line—you can afford to invest. Spend $2 less per day—that's the cost of one less Starbucks coffee or one less soda and crackers from the junk-food machines—and you've got $60 a month. That's enough to plop into an automatic investment plan with a mutual fund.

Still think it's a matter of poverty, not spending? Do this: Start carrying a notebook around with you. Jot down every expense, from the $1 coffee to the $25 you spend filling up your car. Review your notebook after a month. Add up the things that weren't necessities. Vow to cut those by half (or, if you couldn't stand the deprivation, by one-quarter). Put the amount you're no longer spending into savings. Voilà.

❑   **The substitution shopper:** Speaking of shopping, is this what you do when you have a fight with your boss or your spouse? Do you find that you "need" a good shop whenever you're feeling down, as a way of boosting your spirits?

The bad news is your credit card balance is likely to rise faster than your spirits. As a result, you're sentencing yourself to a life of servitude—working harder or more hours to pay your debts, which makes you all the more depressed.

If you need to get rid of your boss or your spouse, stop spending and start saving. What will make you happy now and forever is knowing that you've become financially independent enough to tell whoever is bugging you to shove off.

But shopping really does make you happy? OK, shop. But leave the credit cards at home. Shopping may make you happy, but overspending makes you poor.

❑ **The martyr:** "How can I save for myself when Johnny needs a new soccer uniform and we haven't even gotten close to funding Susie's college account?" you whine. Heavens to Betsy, your honeybunch is wearing a gravy-spotted tie, and you just know that he would be happier and more successful at work if you just sacrificed a little more to get him some nicer duds.

Certainly, it would be nice to think of yourself once in a while, you admit, but how can you when you're so busy being the family caregiver? After all, somebody has to take care of the rest of the family, and no one else has stepped up to the plate to do it. So all of your worldly concerns are going to be put on the back burner until you take care of theirs—today, tomorrow, and forever. Right?

Consider this: if you are strong physically and financially, you can solve a lot more problems for your family than if you're weak. That's precisely why young moms need to balance their long-term financial needs with the pressing day-to-day expenses of managing a young family.

Vow to set some priorities, and make your retirement account one of them. If you are working and have access to a company 401(k) plan, contribute to it. It is, hands down, the best way to save for your retirement needs. If you don't have a 401(k)—if you don't even have a paying job—set up an automatic savings account with a mutual fund (see Chapter 12). Even if all you're saving is $50 a month, you'll have started taking care of yourself and making yourself financially strong. You owe that to yourself and to your kids.

❑ **The princess:** Why save and invest yourself when there's always been someone willing to take care of you? First there was Dad. Then there was your husband. Both of them are kind and thoughtful and wonderful providers.

But what happens if they both predecease you? Women usually live longer than men.

Then there's that other uncomfortable fact of life: About half of marriages end in divorce. Are you prepared to take care of yourself if you're forced to because of death or divorce? Roughly 90 percent of women are going to need to take care of themselves economically at some point in their lives. Think about it.

Then start reading about investments. Put a toe in the market by joining an investment club or starting a monthly investment program with a mutual fund. You can learn about mutual funds in Chapter 8. If you want to join an investment club, you can find information on the Web at www.better-investing.org.

Men

A LTHOUGH MEN USUALLY HAVE MORE MONEY THAN WOMEN, THEY STILL MAKE SOME SURPRISING MIS-takes. Sometimes they invest too aggressively; sometimes they worry too much, second-guessing their best judgment; sometimes they get so caught up in saving and investing that they forget what the money is for. By and large, it appears that the bulk of their problems stem from one thought: This is a game. I've got to win, either for the pure competition or for the spoils. Such thinking produces the following types of investors.

❑ **The unrealistic pessimist:** You go to a cocktail party and start talking to some guy. He's wearing a nice suit, he's confident, and he starts telling you that he's making a killing in the stock market. "Yeah, I doubled my money on Amazon.com in three months," he brags. "Then I bought this little penny stock, and whammo! It tripled in value!"

You stand there quietly, wondering why you've been doing it so wrong. Here you are investing in companies with track records, earnings, sales, and supposedly skilled managers, and what is your portfolio earning? A paltry 10 percent to 15 percent per year, you grouse. "What kind of loser am I? Why didn't I buy that penny stock?" you think. You begin to question your whole investing strategy. You need to be more like *that* guy ... that cocktail-party guy.

You go home, and you buy some of that guy's stock. Maybe you sell some of your boring stocks and mutual funds. When you lose money on those new investments, you know that it's your fault. You're a loser—not a winner like that cocktail-party guy.

Naturally, what the cocktail-party guy didn't mention was that two weeks before he met you, he was downtrodden because his portfolio had declined in value by half, and he was wondering whether he'd have enough cash to make his mortgage. Why didn't he tell you about that? Well, it's not really cocktail-party chatter, is it?

But you should know that anyone who makes a fortune overnight can also lose a fortune overnight. Risk and reward go hand in hand in the financial markets.

If you have thought out a reasonable investment strategy, stick with it. Don't be derailed by a big talker.

❑ **The unrealistic optimist:** You bought a stock figuring that it was going to go to $50. Then lo and behold, it popped up to $65. Based on all of your market knowledge, this is an incredibly high price for this stock. Its price/earnings ratio (see Chapter 5) has never been this high, and you can't imagine why it might be now. And yet, if it went to $65, it could go to $70, right? Maybe you ought to hang on just a little longer and see.

The fact is, the stock could go higher. Or it could go much, much lower. Every time you buy a stock, you should have a target—a price at which you would either sell the stock or reevaluate its prospects before you decide to leave it in your portfolio (see Chapter 6). Don't let emotion—regardless of whether that emotion is fear, greed, or hope—rule your actions.

Financial markets are mathematical. Do the math. Make the evaluation. Live with the idea that you may never sell at the peak. That's OK, as long as you also don't sell at the nadir.

❑ **The ostrich:** You don't have a loss until you sell. Sure, the market price may have dropped, but until you sell, there's hope that the company and the stock will recover, and you will be safe to brag at cocktail parties again. For this reason, many a man holds onto a money-losing stock until it loses everything but its wallpaper value.

Evaluate your stocks once a year. Make reasonable decisions about whether each one is a buy, a hold, or a sell. If you realize that you wouldn't buy a stock today given its future prospects and that there are better opportunities out there, sell it. Take the tax deduction. You'll lose less money and less sleep in the end.

❑ **The tinkerer:** You saw it on *Tool Time.* You do it in your portfolio. Here you have a perfectly functioning item, be it a lawn mower or a stock. But you know that if you just fiddle with it a little bit, you could make it better.

When you're dealing with tools, the worst thing that can happen is you'll have to replace them. When you're dealing with your portfolio, the stakes are considerably higher. But now that you can check your stocks on the Web—and trade for just a few bucks a pop—it's particularly tough to leave well enough alone.

Many tinkerers are particularly apt to sell stocks when they've got a bit of a profit. "Lock that in," they say. Naturally, if the stock keeps rising, they've missed out. Worse still, every time you sell a stock at a profit in a taxable account, you not only have to pay a trading fee, you also pay tax on the gain. If you held the stock for more than a year, that tax will be at capital gains rates, which max out at 20 percent; if you've held it for less than a year, the gain is taxed at your ordinary income tax rates, which are sure to be higher. Either way, to make up for the taxes you pay, you'll have to earn more than a 20 percent return on your next stock purchase just to break even. Don't trade just because you can.

❑ **The believer:** On Wall Street they call some companies "story stocks." They're companies without track records of good sales and earnings, but their managers have a great tale to tell. They've got prospects. It's easy for almost anyone to get caught up in the euphoria—to imagine that this twenty-seven-year-old wunderkind will be the next Bill Gates, capable of carrying you into the realm of the rich and famous. But at some point you've got to look at the numbers. If the numbers don't support the story, you've got to ask yourself whether this stock belongs in your portfolio, regardless of how much faith you have in the tale.

How do you do that? Frankly, it's tough. But plowing along oblivious to the numbers is the investment equivalent of failing to stop and ask directions. If you are not certain how to evaluate a story stock, seek out information on that industry. Read everything you can. Consult experts. If your story stock happens to be in the technology industry, check out Chapter 5. It's got some tips on how to survive and profit in an industry full of fish stories.

❑ **The money-lover:** You invest every dime, often scrimping and saving to do it. And thanks to this superfrugality, you have a lot of money saved and invested. But it's not enough, you theorize. It's never enough. So you work extra hours; you skip vacations; you urge your spouse to do the same. All the while, your riches are growing bigger, and you are growing older.

Before you postpone one more vacation or miss one more baseball game, stop and consider what all this money is for. What are the things in life that you hold precious? Have you saved enough to buy those things? (You can answer that by completing the worksheets in Chapter 3.) In fact, is your emphasis on saving robbing you of enjoying these things? If so, slow down. Step back. Reevaluate your actions.

Too many men work themselves into ulcers, heart attacks, or divorces in a quest to get something that they already had but were too busy working to notice. Evaluate how much money you need for your personal goals. Figure out how close you are to accumulating that amount of money. Then, once you have more than enough, relax. Enjoy it. Spend your time with your family and friends rather than your portfolio. That's what the money is for.

❏ **The fool for love:** OK, you were in that last category. And you know it probably cost you your first marriage. But you also know that your current wealth is the reason all those beautiful young model types are interested in you. You've got to keep it up so this gorgeous girl, twenty years your junior, will agree to marry you and let you buy her a three-carat diamond and a Porsche.

I'm not going to tell you you're wrong. There are definitely women who marry for money. Women who won't marry for money like to call the women who will marry for money "bimbos." It saves us time. After all, the term "women who will marry for money" is so wordy.

So let's say you do get to marry a bimbo. You go home at night and admire her perfect hair, her manicured nails, her sculptured figure. You know you're the most envied man in the room when you walk into a party with her on your arm. You love how she doesn't interrupt when you tell her a long story about your latest success at work. And when you ask her a question, you think it's so cute the way her lips purse before she says, "Huh?"

But keep in mind a few words of wisdom about bimbo Darwinism: While you know twice as much as she does about business and investing, she knows twice as much as you do about the community property laws in your state.

As your mother used to say, "Be careful what you wish for."

chapter 2

Risk and Reward

F INANCIAL PLANNERS tell stories about people who hesitate to invest in the stock market because they fear risk. There are widows who fear that a stock crash could leave them destitute. There are young couples who pine for a new home but worry that an investment loss could kill their chances. And there are people who want to avoid the devastation their parents or grandparents experienced after the 1929 market crash.

Often, however, these fears are rooted in a misunderstanding of what risk is when it comes to the financial markets. Those who understand market risks—and properly evaluate their ability to tolerate them—can supercharge their investment portfolios by embracing a certain amount of uncertainty.

———

Understanding Market Risks

AMES P. KING, A FINANCIAL PLANNER FROM WALNUT CREEK, CALIFORNIA, ILLUSTRATES THIS POINT WITH A riddle: Consider two investments. With the first, you are guaranteed to lose money. Invest $1,000, and you'll lose $1,000. The other could allow you to cash out with an amount ranging from $0 to $5,000 on your $1,000 investment. Which is riskier?

Many individuals would say the riskier investment is the first, because their principal would be in greater jeopardy. But to financial professionals, the first investment is merely stupid—not risky—because it's a sure thing to lose.

In the financial world, risk translates to uncertainty. "It's measured by standard deviation from the norm," says James E. Andelman, a consultant at Ibbotson Associates, a Chicago-based market research and consulting firm. Adds King, "Most individuals measure risk as their chance of loss, but we measure risk by the variability of returns."

In a market that hangs its hat on the close correlation between risk and reward, that's an important distinction. Stocks are considered risky because their prices deviate, sometimes by a lot. In the stock market's worst year, the value of big-company shares fell 43.3 percent. In its best year, they rose 53.9 percent. But even as prices swing wildly, the odds are in your favor over the long haul.

Nothing illustrates the point better than charts compiled by

Ibbotson that show the variability of returns—and total returns—from 1926 through 1998. The summary version: The returns on small-company stocks—which are even more volatile than big-company stocks—have varied by as much as 78 percent in a given decade, whereas the returns on Treasury bills have varied by less than 1 percent. But because the Treasury bill returns are a relative sure thing—there's very little deviation—the rewards are slim.

Consider: If you had invested $1 in the U.S. stock market in 1926 and left it there until 1998, you would have suffered some sickening jolts, including the 1929 market crash and the 1987 minicrash, along the way. In fact, big company stocks lost value in twenty years out of seventy-three, according to Ibbotson. But you also would have enjoyed some years in which your wealth soared. In the end, your $1 would have grown to a stunning $2,350.89.

If on the other hand you had invested that $1 in Treasury bills in 1926, you would have seen only one down year, and the loss would be too small to mention. In all seventy-two others, your return would have inched ahead. Still, because your average annual return would amount to a lackluster 3.7 percent, your $1 would have been worth just $14.94 at the end of 1998. If you factor in inflation and income taxes, T-bills begin to look a great deal like the first investment option in King's riddle.

In fact, every type of investment poses some type of risk. While so-called principal risk, or the chance of losing all or a portion of your initial investment, is the risk that most fledgling investors know about, even instruments that you would call supersafe pose some type of risk. Treasury bonds, for example, pose something called interest-rate risk. (When interest rates rise, the market value of older, relatively low-rate bonds falls.) Bank accounts, certificates of deposit, and Treasury bills pose inflation risk, which is the chance that the after-tax return on your investment won't keep pace with the rate of inflation. That means you lose buying power with every dollar you save.

Still, there's one reason that stocks tend to worry people more:

You never know when the stock market is going to dive. "What if it falls right before I need to sell?" the risk-averse investor asks. The presumption is that your plans would be ruined, your finances devastated. However, the real answer to that question may surprise you. There are very few points in history when you would have been behind by investing in stocks, as long as you left your money invested for at least several years.

Considering Rates
of Return

C ONSIDER THIS: THE AVERAGE ANNUAL RETURN OF BIG-COMPANY STOCKS HAS EXCEEDED 11 PERCENT OVER THE past seventy-three years; the average annual return of long-term government bonds was just over 5 percent during that same period. So what would have happened if you had invested in stocks over a ten-year period but then were unlucky enough to cash out the day that the market took a nosedive? Chances are, you'd still be significantly better off than somebody who invested the same amount in bonds, taking home that steady 5 percent return.

How much better off? If you invested $1,000 and earned 11 percent annually for ten years, you would have accumulated $2,989. If the market took a 30 percent loss before you had a chance to cash out, you'd lose $897 of that, taking home just $2,092. (If you suffered a 40 percent loss, you'd end up with $1,793.)

If you had invested the same amount in bonds or certificates of deposit and earned a 5 percent average annual return instead, you would have cashed out with $1,647 after ten years—signif-icantly less than even the postcrash value of your stock portfolio. In other words, because stocks have higher average returns, you can suffer some serious losses and still end up vastly ahead over the long run. It's important to note that overall market losses this steep—in the 30 percent and 40 percent range—are rare. There have been only two times in history when large-company stocks have lost that much of their value in a single year—once in 1931, and once in 1937. Outside of the Great Depression the worst years for big-company stocks hit during the early 1970s, when stock prices dropped 14.66 percent in 1973 and then 26.47 percent in 1974. After that, prices came roaring back, with big-company stocks posting a 37.2 percent gain in 1975 and a 23.84 percent gain in 1976.

Indeed, when you have a long time horizon, the stock market begins to look downright stable. Whereas there are twenty one-year periods when you would have posted a loss when investing in a broad basket of U.S. stocks, there are only two ten-year periods that were equally bleak. Again, both occurred during the Great Depression.

But these statistics track the market as a whole—not individual stocks. If you buy individual shares, it's not unusual to suffer a 30 percent or 40 percent loss if you happen to buy shares in a company that falls on hard times. Naturally, if that company doesn't recover, neither would the value of your portfolio. That's why you should never invest your entire portfolio in one or two companies' shares. Instead, you diversify your holdings, buying shares in a number of different companies. Diversifying dramatically reduces your risk.

That said, there's only one time when you should not have a diversified basket of U.S. stocks in your portfolio. That's when you don't have time to let the market work for you. In any given year, you have about a one-in-four chance of taking a loss in the stock market. If you plan to invest for only a few years, stocks boil down to a gamble. This is not a wise place to invest your rent money.

But if your time horizon is five years, ten years, or more—as it is for virtually anyone who is investing for retirement—there is a very good chance that putting at least a portion of your money in

The Bare Facts about Variability of Investment Returns

JUST HOW MUCH DO stock returns vary in a given year? Just how likely are you to lose principal from one year to the next? Just how bad could that loss be? Here are a few of the key statistics that tell you how different types of investments have fared over the seventy-three-year period tracked by Ibbotson Associates of Chicago. The chart shows the investment class, the average return, the worst return, and the number of negative-return years, divided by the total number of years tracked, to give you an idea of your chance of loss in any given year.

Asset Class	Average Annual Return	Lowest Annual Return	Number of Negative Years	Total Periods
U.S. small-company stocks	12.41%	-58.01%	22/73	=30.14%
U.S. large-company stocks	11.22%	-43.34%	20/73	=27.39%
Long-term corporate bonds	5.8%	8.09%	16/73	=21.92%
30-year Treasury bonds	5.33%	-9.18%	20/73	=27.39%
Intermediate T-bonds/ notes	5.32%	-5.14%	7/73	= 9.59%
30-day Treasury bills	3.77%	-0.02%	1/73	= 1.37%
International stocks*	12.75%	-23.19	7/28	= 25%

*AS MEASURED BY THE MSCI EAFE INDEX, WHICH HAS TRACKED THE PRICES OF INTERNATIONAL STOCKS SINCE 1970

stocks will boost the performance of your entire portfolio. As your mother used to say, "Nothing ventured, nothing gained." If you take a little risk, you just might gain a lot.

━━━

How Much Investment Risk Can You Tolerate?

W ANT A GRAPHIC ILLUSTRATION OF HOW MUCH RISK YOU CAN HANDLE? HERE'S A QUIZ THAT BRINGS UP MANY of the issues that should affect your risk tolerance and your investment strategies.

In a nutshell, it will show you that you can take more risk in your investment portfolio when you have less risk in your life. Your age, your earnings capacity, and just how nervous you get when the value of your investments drops sharply also have an impact.

Q U I Z

How Much Risk Can You Take?

1 My age is between:
(a) twenty and thirty-five.
(b) thirty-six and forty-five.
(c) forty-six and fifty-five.
(d) fifty-six and sixty-five.
(e) sixty-six and ninety-nine.

2 I have a stable job in a growing industry. I imagine I'll:
(a) continue to work for my present employer unless I

21

get offered a higher-paying job, which is very likely in my industry.

(b) work for my present employer for the rest of my career, because I like it here and the company is growing enough to provide me with some opportunity for advancement.

(c) work here as long as I can, because I don't know what else I'd do.

(d) switch jobs soon. The boredom is killing me.

(e) get fired any day now. I've never been good at this work, and as time goes on, I get worse.

3 Over the next five to ten years, my salary and overall earnings will:

(a) probably grow significantly.

(b) most likely grow steadily—at least as fast as inflation.

(c) stay relatively stable.

(d) possibly decrease somewhat.

(e) decrease significantly.

4 I have a spouse who:

(a) loves me and earns enough to support us both.

(b) earns almost as much as I do and doesn't mind sharing it.

(c) earns a good living.

(d) works part-time.

(e) stays home with our children.

5 I (we) have always lived:

(a) on significantly less than we earn. That's allowed us to save 20 percent or more of our income each year.

(b) well within our means. We save close to 10 percent of our income.

(c) modestly, but we haven't been able to save much of what we earn.

(d) to the outer edges of our income, spending every dime and borrowing a few dimes here and there, too.

(e) on credit.

6 The following number of people rely on me for their financial welfare:

(a) zero.

(b) one.

(c) two.

(d) three.

(e) four or more.

7 The number of years remaining until I expect to retire is:

(a) twenty-five or more.

(b) fifteen to twenty-four.

(c) five to fourteen.

(d) less than five.

(e) none—I'm currently retired.

8 My net worth (the value of my assets minus my debts) is:

(a) more than $350,000.

(b) $150,001 to $350,000.

(c) $50,001 to $150,000.

(d) $15,001 to $50,000.

(e) less than $15,000.

9 The amount I have saved in nonretirement assets equals:

(a) more than two years' salary.

(b) one to two years' salary.

(c) seven months' to one year's salary.

(d) two to six months' salary.

(e) one month's salary or less.

10 I (we) have life insurance that:
   (a) is more than adequate to take care of my family's financial needs if anything happens to me or my spouse.
   (b) I believe would be adequate to cover my family's financial needs in the event that something happened to me or my spouse.
   (c) would pay off the mortgage but would not provide much else.
   (d) would help us survive for a year or two.
   (e) is inadequate (or nonexistent).

11 I (we) have disability insurance that:
   (a) is more than adequate to take care of my family's financial needs if either my spouse or I become disabled for any amount of time.
   (b) is adequate as long as the disability is not particularly long-term. In other words, it will cover us as long as I'm not out of work for more than six months to a year.
   (c) would tide us over for a while, but we'd have to cut back.
   (d) would cover some but not all of our expenses, and not for any length of time.
   (e) . . . . Disability insurance?

12 I have health insurance that provides:
   (a) great coverage for me and my family.
   (b) adequate coverage for me and my family.
   (c) catastrophic coverage, after I pay a significant deductible.
   (d) good coverage only if I see certain doctors, in whom I have little faith.
   (e) I don't have health insurance.

13 When I buy stock investments, I:

(a) contemplate what the money is for and feel comfortable leaving it alone until I need it for that specific goal. As a result, I may not look at the market
value for months.

(b) analyze what I'm buying and why and usually feel
capable of sticking with the program. But I have to
know what the market is doing on a very regular—
ideally daily—basis so I can reanalyze and consider
whether I was wrong the first time.

(c) try to match my investments with my goals, but I'm
never quite certain that I've got the mix just right.

(d) stick with them unless they start to decline in value.
Then I get nervous and second-guess myself, which
sometimes causes me to trade at all the wrong
times.

(e) watch them like a hawk, because I don't want to
lose any principal.

14 The majority of my financial goals are:

(a) very long-term—things that are at least fifteen to
twenty years in the future.

(b) fairly long-term—things that are between ten and
fifteen years in the future.

(c) mixed—I have some relatively short-term goals,
like establishing an emergency fund; some medium-
term goals, like buying a house; and some long-
term goals, like retirement, which is decades from
now.

(d) mostly short- to medium-term—my kids are in (or
about to enroll in) college, and my retirement is
looming on the not-too-distant horizon.

(e) very short-term—I'm in retirement, and my main
goal is to have my current savings provide enough
monthly income to live on.

15 My family and friends are:

(a) very supportive. They're the type of people who would let me move in with them if I happened to lose all of my money in a stock market reversal or a bad commodity trade.

(b) pretty supportive. They'd lend me money and—in a pinch—let me move back home if my finances crumbled due to some event that was outside of my control.

(c) supportive but not financially capable of helping a great deal.

(d) not supportive, but as long as I don't ask for anything, they leave me alone.

(e) a constant drain on my assets. They don't provide support, ever; they just ask for it.

Scoring

GIVE YOURSELF FIVE POINTS for every (a) answer; four points for each (b); three points for each (c); two points for each (d); and one point for each (e). Your score:

_____

❑ **65 to 75:** You probably have the money and the inclination to take lots of risks. High-risk investments include aggressive-growth stocks, start-up companies, commodities, junk bonds, international stocks, stock options, and investment real estate. However, be sure to diversify at least some of your portfolio into safer investments. You could regret your high risk tolerance if you lost everything.

❑ **51 to 64:** You have an above-average tolerance for risk and probably enough time and income to cover some investment losses. Investors in this category are wise to mix high-risk and medium-risk options.

❑ **36 to 50:** You have an average tolerance for risk but don't like to gamble. Make a point of dividing your assets by goal and then investing those assets in quality stocks, bonds, notes, and money market funds that address your needs while allowing you to sleep soundly at night. Since you're likely to have a wide range of goals—from beefing up an emergency fund to maximizing returns on a retirement account—expect that your assets will be mixed among high-, low-, and medium-risk options.

❑ **21 to 35:** You have below-average tolerance for risk, either because of your age or because of your income and family circumstances. Comfortable investments for you would probably include your home, high-quality bonds, government-backed securities, and federally insured savings accounts. But make sure you keep at least some of your retirement savings in stocks. After all, even if you're retired or near retirement, you're probably not near death. That means at least part of your retirement dollars are long-term investments. Keeping a portion of your long-term investments in stocks should allow that portion of your portfolio to grow as fast as (or faster than) inflation over time. That allows you to maintain long-term buying power.

❑ **15 to 20:** You have virtually no tolerance for risk. Look for investments that have government backing, such as bank and thrift certificates of deposit, Treasury bills, bonds, and notes. As you learn more about investing—or as your life circumstances change for the better—check your risk tolerance again. You may find that a good grounding in investment education will boost your comfort with taking some investment risks, which should help improve your long-term financial health.

chapter 3

Your Starting Point

J OHN HAS BEEN INVESTING for about five years—long enough to know that a bull market is a market in which stock prices are climbing strongly and a bear market is one in which they're languishing. The only trouble is, he's never quite sure whether he's got the bull by the horns or is about to be mauled by the bear. With his life savings riding on the answer, he says that he approaches each day with nail-biting nervousness.

"Every time the market climbs, I'm wondering whether I should sell to lock in my profits. When it drops, I wonder whether I should sell to cut my losses," he says. "Most of the time, I don't actually do anything—other than worry about it."

Anecdotal evidence indicates that John, a broker who asked not to be named for fear of losing all his clients, isn't alone. Investing makes many people nervous, because they know that their future financial health can hinge on the choices they make. And there are a huge variety of highly complicated options confronting investors every day.

However, investing doesn't have to be difficult or nerve-racking. In fact, wise investing is simple, once you understand a few key facts.

What are they? First and foremost is this: The goal of this game is not to accumulate more money than God. It is not getting a 20 percent or 40 percent or even 50 percent investment return. It is not bragging at cocktail parties. It is this and only this: having the amount of money you need when you need it.

Make this your mantra. If you ever wonder about whether you are investing wisely, ask yourself this question: "Will I have the amount of money that I need when I need it with my present investment strategy?" If the answer is yes, you're doing it right. If the answer is no, you need to change something. It is that simple.

Allocating Assets
Based on Goals

S O HOW DO YOU MAKE SURE THAT YOU HAVE THE MONEY YOU NEED WHEN YOU NEED IT? YOU START BY PUTTING your assets in appropriate investment categories, based on your goals. In marketspeak, this process is called "asset allocation." Although pundits make this process sound complex—as if there's some secret formula to doing it right that they know and you don't—the reality is it's a simple process.

Identifying Investment Categories

ASSET ALLOCATION BEGINS with categorizing investments into five basic types. These categories are based on what the investment does for you rather than what the investment is. By categorizing in this fashion, you can easily allocate your assets into broad investment groups.

1 Investments that safeguard your principal
2 Investments that provide you with income
3 Investments that promise strong growth of your principal
4 Investments that protect you from the ravages of inflation
5 Investments that allow you to speculate

If you are like most people, you will need investments in three of these five categories. If inflation makes you nervous, you may choose to invest in four. But unless you are very young or very rich, you should skip investments in the fifth category. That's simply because investments that allow you to speculate are more like gambling than investing. If (or when) you have enough money that you can take a pot of cash and roll the dice—knowing that you've got just as good a chance of losing it all as you do of doubling your money overnight—then invest in that last category. Until then, stick to the first four.

Why do you want investments in at least the first three of these categories? Mainly because nearly everyone has a financial goal that is best addressed by one of these three investment types.

For instance, every one of us would be wise to keep some money safe to handle life's curves—that's anything from unexpected medical expenses or car repairs to the loss of a job. Income investments, meanwhile, are perfect for two things: to fund short- and mid-range goals and to provide extra income to

31

handle daily living expenses. The people who can most benefit from income investments can be anyone from a retiree to a young family intent on buying something big in the near future, such as a house or a car.

Meanwhile, anyone who hopes to retire someday needs some growth investments, because growth investments tend to grow substantially faster than the rate of inflation. Therefore, they increase your buying power over time. Increase your buying power enough and you can finance massive goals, like the urge to quit your job and live off your savings in comfort for forty years or so.

Who needs inflation-protecting investments? Mainly people who worry a lot. The biggest proponents of having a large portion of your assets in inflation-protecting investments are people who also have stored gold, guns, and canned goods in their bomb shelters. In reality, inflation has averaged just about 3 percent per year since 1926. You should be able to earn significantly more than that on your invested cash.

Still, although it is easy to make light of the "end is near" crowd, there have been times in history when protecting yourself from inflation was a remarkably good idea—the 1970s, for example. Even though most experts don't advise that you keep a lot of your investment assets in inflation-protection-type securities, there is one investment that does a great job protecting you from inflation and provides other comforts as well. You'll learn about it in the next chapter: Diversification.

In fact, the only hard part about asset allocation is deciding how much money to put in each type of investment. Frankly, that's not tricky or complex, it's simply time-consuming. Why? To do it right, you have to consider precisely what you are saving for and how much you need to address each goal. Once you do that, your assets practically allocate themselves.

Identifying Financial Goals

SO NOW IT'S TIME to think about what you want in life and just what your goals and dreams are going to cost you. To help, the rest of this chapter talks about seven common goals—having emergency money, saving for a car, buying a house, paying for college, creating a "freedom" fund, saving for retirement, and generating savings that will produce income to live on.

You may have other goals, but chances are they're similar enough to at least one of these that you can use the discussion and worksheets provided with each of these goals to help you figure out the right amount to save. The end of each section will discuss what types of investments best suit that goal and will direct you to the part of this book that gives more information about those types of investments.

DOING THE NUMBERS

Putting Dollars and Dreams Together

Goal: Emergency Money

PREPARE TO GET DEPRESSED. To appropriately address your need for emergency cash, you need to mull a variety of worst-case scenarios—all of the things that you are not financially prepared to handle, whether that's the loss of a job or the loss of a spouse. Then you need to consider what other resources you could tap to tide you over.

The reason you have to consider your other resources in the same breath as your disasters is a simple one. Emergency money needs to be kept in very safe investments that pose little risk to your principal—things like bank accounts, money market mutual funds, and short-term Treasury bills. However, as you'll learn in the next chapter, this type of investment also produces very little return. Normally, in fact, the yields are so slim with super-safe investments that the after-tax return on your money is unlikely to keep pace with inflation. That means you lose buying power over time.

Does that mean you shouldn't have an emergency fund? Not at all. If you are likely to suffer some type of emergency and have no better way to address it, an emergency fund is invaluable. You just don't want to keep more money in emergency savings than absolutely necessary.

To dedicate the right amount to emergency savings, you must handicap your risks and quantify the potential cost. To clarify: You need to consider the type of emergency that you're most likely to suffer. Then, figure, as closely as you can, just how much money you'd need to muddle through it.

Like what, you ask?

Disaster Central: Delineating Potential Emergencies

❑ **Car repairs.** If you're just starting out in life, your biggest risk may be the junker in your driveway. (You know that if you lost your job, Mom and Dad would let you move back in. While that's not ideal, it's better than living on the street. But if your car breaks down—again—you'll have to repair it, and quick, or you'll lose your job and end up living with Mom and Dad.) How much do you need to have in emergency savings to fix the car? The best way to figure it is to consider four things:

1 What has it cost to repair the car in the past?

2   What would it cost to put a down payment on a new car if the current repair cost is way more than you're willing to spend?

3   Do you have borrowing power—an unused line of credit or credit card that could be tapped to pay the bill if necessary (keeping in mind that you'd then have to work hard to pay it off so you wouldn't end up paying stunning amounts in interest)?

4   How averse are you to riding the bus? The seriously bus-averse are likely to need more—somewhere between $500 to $1,000—to deal with car repairs, whereas those with reliable cars and/or bus passes may dedicate significantly less to this goal.

How much do you need? Make your best guess:

$_____

❏   **Home repairs.** You fell in love with that 1914 bungalow. The chipped paint and broken windows ensured that you got it for a price that you could afford—although just barely. But then the water heater blew. It was either fix it, take cold showers, or start wearing very strong perfume. Now from the noise that's coming from the furnace, you're thinking that'll go next. How much emergency money you ought to set aside for this repair hinges on the answers to the following questions: How many blankets do I have? Is the furnace in only slightly worse shape than the roof? How do I feel about camping?

It's worth mentioning that if you have a newer house that's in decent shape, home repairs aren't generally emergencies, they're planned events. But if the previous story describes you, you'll need to do a little shopping at your local hardware store or Home Depot to get a read on how much you'll need. The result:

$_____

❏   **Short-term disability**. Do you have insurance that would pay you monthly income if you were unable to work for

35

an extended period because of some disabling injury or illness? Most people who pay into the Social Security system through payroll taxes do. However, Social Security disability covers just long-term problems—those that last six months or more. (Then, too, if you're a high-income wage earner, it's likely to replace only a small fraction of your wages.) The best way to deal with the risk of a short-term disability is to insure against it, preferably through a policy offered through your employee benefit plan at work. However, if your disability insurance has a waiting period—or if the monthly payment would be so low that it wouldn't cover your day-to-day fixed expenses—you might want to save a little extra money to fill the gaps. How much? To answer, you'd be wise to consider your personal risk of disability. If you are in construction and a broken leg would put you out of work, your risks are much higher than if you're like me, a writer, who could be in a full-body cast and still be able to dictate a story. Additionally, your need for emergency money will be affected by just how much sick leave your employer provides. If your employer allows an indefinite amount of sick leave, your need for an emergency fund to handle short-term disability evaporates completely. On the other hand, if you don't get any sick leave and you're in a relatively high-risk profession, you might want at least a month's wages in the bank.

$

❑   **Job loss.** For most adults, losing a job is the biggest potential emergency that can't be addressed through the purchase of life, health, or disability insurance. It is also the primary reason why some financial planners suggest having six months' worth of wages in emergency savings. However, as we've already discussed, keeping a big horde of cash in low-yielding investments might not be the best thing to do for your long-term financial health—unless, of course, your risk of job loss is high and the potential repercussions of that job loss are great. For instance, you work in an industry (or for a company) that's undergoing major change. Layoffs are rampant. You are the only wage earner in your household, and your monthly expenses are so close

36

to your monthly income that even a short period of unemployment would send your household into a tailspin. If that's you, load up on emergency savings. On the other hand, if you have a relatively stable job in an industry that's growing and you have the reputation and skills to find other work quickly, your need for emergency savings may be minimal.

$ \$_____ $

❑ **Death of a spouse.** The death of a wage-earning spouse is not only a tragedy, it's a financial emergency. However, it is not one that can be adequately addressed through emergency savings. That's simply because the gap between what you as the surviving spouse would be able to earn and what you'd need is likely to be far too great, particularly if you have young children. (Indeed, even if your stay-at-home spouse dies, you are likely to face serious economic consequences. Consider adding the cost of hiring a full-time baby-sitter, cook, and housekeeper to your monthly budget, and then give your stay-at-home spouse a grateful kiss.)

For this risk, you need life insurance. To determine how much, consider what would happen if you or your spouse died. How much of a gap would there be between what you need and what you earn? How long would you need to fill that gap? Add those figures up, and then go to the Internet (or a life insurance agent) to buy a policy big enough to fill the gap.

❑ **Total emergency fund needed.** Before you simply add all the numbers in the previous paragraphs (plus a bit more for unmentioned emergencies that you may not anticipate), remember that no one (except the biblical Job) is likely to suffer every emergency imaginable back-to-back or at the same time. Put aside an amount that's sufficient to handle your biggest emergency. Once that crisis is over, vow to quickly replenish the emergency savings.

$ \$_____ $

For appropriate investments for your emergency money, look in the section "Investing for Safety" in Chapter 4, "Diversification."

Goal: Saving for a Car

OF ALL FINANCIAL GOALS, figuring out how much you need to save for a car—and how to invest that money—is among the easiest. That's because you already have a clear idea of the type of car you want. You know—or easily can find out—roughly how much it costs. In addition, you can fairly accurately predict when you want to make your purchase. (Of course, the reality of how much you've got saved could cause you to change the purchase date or model of the car.)

You also know just how precious this goal is to you, so you can make some reasonable determinations about how much investment risk you're willing to take in the pursuit of that goal. If, for example, you wouldn't fall into a deep depression if your Porsche purchase had to be delayed because the stock market had a bad stretch, you could gamble a bit and put part—or even all—of your auto-purchase money into domestic stocks.

On the other hand, if you are trying to buy a new Honda because your old one is nearly worn out and you're worried about your ability to get safely to and from work, you'd be wise to invest more conservatively. You'd want to put your money in high-grade fixed-income investments that would mature at the point that you wanted to make your purchase. (If you prefer to invest through mutual funds, a medium-term bond fund that has a fairly stable net asset value would do the trick.)

The only other issue is how you want to pay for the car: Will you buy it outright with cash, lease it, or put some money down and finance the rest? Your answer will determine just how much you need to save. How much do you figure?

$

Now, assuming that you need to save that money over time, we'll need to do a little math to determine just how much you need to save each month to reach your goal. You've written the amount that you think you'll need. Do you have current savings? If so, log the amount you've already got on the following line and multiply that number by the appropriate multiplier in the chart below. The appropriate multiplier is the one that corresponds to the amount of time you have to reach your goal and the interest rate you believe you'll earn on your money in the meantime. You'll notice there are only four interest rates listed, ranging from 3 percent to 6 percent. In a normal market, this is the best you can expect to do on relatively short-term savings (anything from one to five years). If you earn more than this, celebrate. It means you can buy the car sooner or with a bigger down payment or get more extras. (A note of advice—the less time you have until the purchase, the lower your likely rate of return.)

Your current savings:

$_____ x _____ = $_____

(amount I have) (multiplier)   (future value of my savings)

Time to Goal			Rate of Return	
	3%	4%	5%	6%
1 year	1.03	1.04	1.05	1.06
2 years	1.062	1.083	1.105	1.127
3 years	1.094	1.127	1.161	1.197
4 years	1.127	1.173	1.221	1.270
5 years	1.162	1.221	1.283	1.349

Now subtract the amount you need from the amount you have. This is the gap that you'll need to fill with additional monthly savings. Gap:

$_____

How much will that cost you each month? Since this is a relatively short-term goal, the interest you'll earn on your monthly savings is not likely to amount to much. As a result, we can save the fancy math and go for something simple: Divide your number by the number of months you have to go. In other words, if you figure you'll need $1,000 more than you've got and you want to buy the car in two years, divide $1,000 by 24 months. You must save $41.67 per month to reach your goal. Your result:

$

Appropriate investments for auto-purchase money can range from very low risk to relatively high risk. Low-risk investments, such as those mentioned in Chapter 4 in the section "Investing for Safety," are appropriate if you need the car very soon and you can't stand the idea of delaying the purchase because you took a loss on your investments. You can choose moderate-risk investments, including short- to medium-term bonds, bond funds, and stock mutual funds, if you have a little more time and a slight market loss won't devastate you.

If the car is a luxury and you can handle delaying the purchase, you can invest in growth investments, including stock mutual funds or even individual stocks. If you're lucky, these investments could return significantly more than you planned, leaving you with a bigger down payment or a better car. If you're not lucky, you may have to go for the Lumina rather than the Lexus. If this is your biggest problem in life, count yourself lucky.

Goal: Buying a House

THE PROCESS OF FIGURING OUT how much you ought to save for a house and how you ought to invest that money is very similar to the process you go through when saving for a car. You simply need to consider what kind of house you want and what it costs.

If you want to buy with a traditional 20 percent down payment—which will net you the lowest interest rate—you multiply the cost of the house by 20 percent. That's the amount that you need to save. You can't possibly save that much before you buy? If the market's right and your credit is good, you can probably get a loan with a low down payment. But you'll end up paying a somewhat higher rate of interest if you do. However, even in the best of circumstances, you'll need somewhere between 3 percent and 5 percent of the purchase price in cash to handle a down payment and closing costs. Enter the estimated down payment amount for your home:

$_____

Where is that money going to come from? Two sources: the money you already have saved and invested, and the additional savings you'll set aside each month. To figure out how much you need to save monthly, you first need to know what your current savings will be worth in the future. To do that, multiply your current savings by the appropriate figure in the chart on page 42. The less time you have before you want to buy, the more conservative you need to be about the rate of return you're likely to earn on your money.

Your current savings:

$_____ x _____ = $_____

                (multiplier)   (future value of my savings)

Goal: House (future value of savings)							
Time to Goal							Rate of Return
3%	4%	5%	6%	7%	8%	9%	10%
1 year 1.03	1.04	1.05	1.06	1.07	1.08	1.09	1.10
2 years 1.062	1.083	1.105	1.127	1.150	1.173	1.196	1.220
3 years 1.094	1.127	1.161	1.197	1.233	1.270	1.309	1.348
4 years 1.127	1.173	1.221	1.270	1.322	1.376	1.431	1.489
5 years 1.162	1.221	1.283	1.349	1.418	1.490	1.566	1.645
6 years 1.196	1.271	1.349	1.432	1.520	1.613	1.712	1.818
7 years 1.233	1.322	1.418	1.520	1.630	1.747	1.873	2.007
8 years 1.271	1.376	1.490	1.614	1.748	1.892	2.049	2.218
9 years 1.309	1.432	1.567	1.714	1.874	2.049	2.241	2.450
10 years 1.349	1.491	1.647	1.819	2.010	2.220	2.451	2.707

Now subtract what you'll have from the amount you want. The result is the amount you need to save between now and then.

$_____

How much do you need to save each month to accumulate that amount? Assuming that your home purchase is more than a few years away, you'll want to figure in the impact of investment returns on your monthly savings to come up with a fairly accurate estimate. (It's only "fairly accurate" because you're often guessing on the investment return. Frankly, you're probably guessing a bit about the time you have before you buy, too. Realize that these are educated guesses that ought to get you close to your goal. In the end, you might have a bit more or a bit less than you planned.)

$_____ x _____ = $_____
(amount you want) (multiplier)   (additional monthly
                                            savings needed)

Goal: House (additional savings needed) Time to Goal							Rate of Return
3%	**4%**	**5%**	**6%**	**7%**	**8%**	**9%**	**10%**
3 years .0266	.0262	.0258	.0254	.0250	.0247	.0243	.0239
4 years .0196	.0192	.0188	.0184	.0181	.0177	.0174	.0170
5 years .0155	.0151	.0147	.0143	.0140	.0136	.0133	.0129
6 years .0127	.0123	.0119	.0116	.0112	.0109	.0105	.0102
7 years .0107	.0103	.0100	.0096	.0092	.0089	.0086	.0083
8 years .0092	.0088	.0085	.0081	.0078	.0075	.0071	.0068
9 years .0081	.0077	.0073	.0070	.0067	.0063	.0060	.0057
10 years .0071	.0068	.0064	.0061	.0058	.0055	.0052	.0049

To find the right investment mix for your home savings, you need to go through virtually the same thought process as the person who wants to buy a car. Consider: Is this a necessity or a luxury? How devastating will it be if the home purchase is delayed, or if you have to buy a little less house than you planned?

You'd be wise to invest in a mixture of income and growth investments. That will keep some of your principal relatively safe while giving you a chance at getting your nest egg to grow faster than the rate of inflation—a virtual must if you ever want to get in that home. However, since your goal is relatively short term, you would be wise to stick with mutual funds rather than trying to pick individual stocks for the growth portion of your portfolio. Mutual funds can provide you with much greater diversification of your assets, which usually smooths out the big bumps in market value.

Goal: Paying for College

THERE'S ONLY ONE PROBLEM with figuring out how much money your kids are going to need for college: your kids. The darned things just aren't born with labels reading "Destined for Harvard" or "Community College, Here I Come!" Naturally, the difference between paying for Harvard and paying for a community college amounts to a fortune. In fact, most middle-income parents could probably pay for community colleges—and even state universities—as they go, since many of those schools cost about the same per semester as it costs to send the kids to summer camp. The cost of Harvard? Brace yourself: Tuition alone was more than $26,000 in the 2001–2002 academic year.

Unfortunately, the best time to save is when the children are tiny (that allows compound interest to work and makes the job of saving enough significantly easier on you). But when they're young, you have no idea what school you're saving for, so you aren't going to know whether you are saving too much or not enough. What do you do? You guess.

If you went to an Ivy League school and thought it was the best thing on the planet, you might want to save for Ivy League tuition to give your child that option. To get an idea of what that will cost, go to the College Board's Web page at www.college-board.org or buy the annual *College Cost & Financial Aid Handbook,* which gives advice on financial aid and spells out the cost of tuition, room, board, and books at 2,700 U.S. colleges and universities.

If, on the other hand, you paid for your own education and thought that the corresponding independence was worth its weight in gold, your education savings goals may be significantly more modest. Obviously, if you expect your children to pay a significant portion of the cost, you'll need to save less than you would if you wanted to finance their education yourself. In any event, you need to pick a number. Weigh the factors you consider important and decide how much assistance you plan to give each child. Then use the following chart and worksheet to figure out just how much you need to save each month to have that amount in the future. If you have more than one child, add the numbers to determine how much to put in the college account each month to finance education for the whole family. A quick note: Unless you are very well-heeled, save this money in your name, not in your children's names. That will give them a better chance of qualifying for student aid later, and it will allow you to keep control of the cash—just in case Junior turns out to be irresponsible and wants to go to Europe (or the Maserati dealer) rather than to school.

If you already have money set aside for college, use the worksheet in the preceding section "Buying a House" to determine what your current savings will be worth in the future. Then subtract the result from the total dollar amount you need to save

Goal: College								
Time to Goal							**Rate of Return**	
	3%	**4%**	**5%**	**6%**	**7%**	**8%**	**9%**	**10%**
3 years	.0266	.0262	.0258	.0254	.0250	.0247	.0243	.0239
4 years	.0196	.0192	.0188	.0184	.0181	.0177	.0174	.0170
5 years	.0155	.0151	.0147	.0143	.0140	.0136	.0133	.0129
6 years	.0127	.0123	.0119	.0116	.0112	.0109	.0105	.0102
7 years	.0107	.0103	.0100	.0096	.0092	.0089	.0086	.0083
8 years	.0092	.0088	.0085	.0081	.0078	.0075	.0071	.0068
9 years	.0081	.0077	.0073	.0070	.0067	.0063	.0060	.0057
10 years	.0071	.0068	.0064	.0061	.0058	.0055	.0052	.0049
11 years	.0064	.0060	.0057	.0054	.0050	.0047	.0045	.0042
12 years	.0058	.0054	.0051	.0048	.0044	.0041	.0039	.0036
13 years	.0052	.0049	.0046	.0042	.0039	.0037	.0034	.0031
14 years	.0048	.0044	.0041	.0038	.0035	.0032	.0030	.0027
15 years	.0044	.0041	.0037	.0034	.0031	.0029	.0026	.0024
16 years	.0041	.0037	.0034	.0031	.0028	.0026	.0023	.0021
17 years	.0038	.0034	.0031	.0028	.0026	.0023	.0021	.0019

WORKSHEET

College Cost Calculator

I want to give _____ for college: $_____
        (child's name)   (dollar amount)

Number of years before this child is old enough to enroll: _____

$_____ x _____ = $_____
(amount you want)   (multiplier from chart)   (monthly savings required)

I want to give _____ for college: $_____
        (child's name)   (dollar amount)

Number of years before this child is old enough to enroll: _____

$_____ x _____ = $_____
(amount you want)   (multiplier from chart)   (monthly savings required)

I want to give _____ for college: $_____
        (child's name)   (dollar amount)

Number of years before this child is old enough to enroll: _____

$_____ x _____ = $_____
(amount you want)   (multiplier from chart)   (monthly savings required)

I want to give _____ for college: $_____
        (child's name)   (dollar amount)

Number of years before this child is old enough to enroll: _____

$_____ x _____ = $_____
(amount you want)   (multiplier from chart)   (monthly savings required)

Total amount of monthly savings needed = $_____
                              (sum of monthly savings for all children)

(the final space on the next line) before you start with these worksheets.

Appropriate investments for your kids' college savings depend on how long they have before enrolling. If you're saving for a teenager, be relatively conservative. You can put some money in stocks and other growth investments, but not a lot. Most of your savings should go in short- and medium-term income investments that will mature when your child is ready to enroll. On the other hand, if you're saving for a toddler, you can be aggressive. Put the bulk of your savings in stocks and very little (if any) in fixed-income investments.

If you have several children—some in high school and some in diapers—you'll want a broad mix of investments, so you'll have some money in relatively stable investments to ensure the funds are there for the high schooler and some money in stocks to help the baby.

Goal: More Freedom/Options

LET'S SAY YOU'RE YOUNG. You don't have kids. You are happy in your apartment. You don't need a fancy car. You could save money, but why? Here's a thought: Buy yourself future freedom. Think about your future life and what you, as a person, hold dear. Do you want, for example, the ability to stay home and raise kids (assuming, of course, that you'll one day have them)? Would you like to know that if you someday work for a complete jerk, you could quit and survive for a while without an income? Do you imagine that you may want to retire early? Or take summer-long vacations with the man/woman of your dreams (someday, after you meet him/her, naturally)?

If so, you're in a great spot. You can save today for goals you may have at some point in the future. How diligently you save now should depend on the likelihood of these future goals. For instance, if you know you love kids and you'd want to spend at least a few years raising them at home, save diligently. You have nothing to lose and great freedom to gain. But as it is virtually impossible to put a dollar amount on a goal that doesn't yet exist, you shouldn't torture yourself trying to figure the right amount to save and invest each month. Instead, figure out an amount you can afford to save. Have that amount automatically deducted from your paycheck or checking account. Invest it aggressively—after all, you have plenty of time to wait out market swings, since you haven't even figured out what the money is for yet. And then, aside from an annual investment checkup (something you need to do with all your investments), forget about it. One day you'll wake up and realize this money you've got gives you options that your friends don't have. That's a nice feeling.

When investing this money, go for broke. Read Chapter 5, "Picking Individual Stocks," and think about international investing (Chapter 10) as well. If you're not wild about picking and choosing individual stocks or simply don't have the time to do it, check out Chapter 8, "Mutual Funds."

Goal: Retirement

TRYING TO FIGURE OUT the right amount to save for retirement is tricky. That's simply because before you can possibly know how much you need to save for retirement, you need to know how much you're going to spend in retirement. That means you have to draw up an estimated retirement budget. How? By looking at today's budget and imagining how life will change when you're no longer working.

Will your house be paid off by then? If so, deduct the cost of the mortgage, but not the cost of repairs. Do you plan to golf every day? If so, add in the cost of greens fees. If you're saving diligently each month, you can also scratch that amount from the budget. Retirement is the spending phase of your life. Then there are a few things that are impossible to figure, such as how much you're going to spend on medicine. Figure that you'll buy some health insurance, and leave yourself a little cushion—just in case.

When you're done, you'll have come up with an estimated amount that you expect to spend each month in retirement. We're going to adjust it for inflation by multiplying it by the appropriate number in the following chart. You'll note there's only one inflation rate given. That's because inflation has averaged slightly over 3 percent over the past seventy-two years. Since this is a long-term question, long-term averages are reasonable numbers to use. (If you want to play with other inflation numbers, there are numerous retirement calculators on the Internet. One of the better ones is at www.familymoney.com.)

$\$$_____ x _____ = $\$$_____

(monthly budget) (multiplier) (inflation-adjusted budget)

Goal: Retirement (inflation-adjusted budget)	
Time to Goal	3% Average Annual Inflation Rate
5 years	1.159
10 years	1.344
15 years	1.558
20 years	1.806
25 years	2.094
30 years	2.427
35 years	2.814
40 years	3.262

Now that you have an inflation-adjusted number, you need to realize that your retirement income is likely to come from three sources: your savings, a company pension (if you have one), and Social Security. If you qualify for Social Security but don't know how much monthly income to expect from it, call the agency and request an earnings and benefit statement. (The agency can be reached at 800-772-1213.) The agency should send you a statement automatically each year. Realize that the farther you are from retirement age, the less accurate this statement will be. But it's a start.

If you also qualify for a defined benefit plan at work—that's the type that pays monthly benefits for life—call your company and get an estimate of what to expect there, too. You can subtract both of those monthly amounts from the amount that you need before you figure out how much you must save.

Your final step is to determine just how much your current retirement savings will generate in monthly income. You can use the multipliers in the following chart to come up with a good guesstimate.

$_____ x _____ = $_____
(current savings) (multiplier   (future value of
                     from chart)   your savings)

Goal: Retirement (future value of savings)							
Time to Retirement				**Estimated Rate of Return**			
5%	**6%**	**7%**	**8%**	**9%**	**10%**	**11%**	**12%**
5 years 1.28	1.35	1.42	1.49	1.57	1.64	1.73	1.82
10 years 1.65	1.82	2.01	2.22	2.45	2.71	2.99	3.30
15 years 2.11	2.45	2.85	3.31	3.84	4.45	5.17	5.99
20 years 2.71	3.31	4.04	4.93	6.01	7.32	8.93	10.89
25 years 3.48	4.46	5.72	7.34	9.41	12.06	15.45	19.79
30 years 4.47	6.02	8.12	10.94	14.73	19.84	26.71	35.95
35 years 5.73	8.12	11.51	16.29	23.06	32.64	46.18	65.31
40 years 7.35	10.96	16.31	24.27	36.11	53.70	79.83	118.65

Now, just to be very safe, multiply that figure by 6 percent to determine just how much annual income your nest egg will throw off without dipping into the principal. Enter the result here:

$_____

Is this less or more than what you figure you'd still need after accounting for your company pension and Social Security? If it's more, you've done enough. You can save more to boost your retirement lifestyle (or to handle any future contingencies that you may not have imagined today), or you can relax. If it's less, you need to save more.

Determining how much more is a two-step process. First, multiply the amount of your monthly shortfall—that's what you expect to need minus what you'll have from your current savings, company pension, and Social Security—by 207. Result:

$_____

Now multiply that number by the appropriate multiplier from the chart below—the one that most closely corresponds to the number of years you have until retirement and the rate of return you expect to earn on your money.

$_____ x _____ = $_____

(your savings gap) (multiplier   (required monthly
                    from chart)   savings)

| Goal: Retirement (required monthly savings) | | | | | | | |
Time to Goal							Rate of Return
	5%	6%	7%	8%	9%	10%	11%	12%
5 years	.0147	.0143	.0140	.0136	.0133	.0129	.0126	.0122
10 years	.0064	.0061	.0058	.0055	.0052	.0049	.0046	.0043
15 years	.0037	.0034	.0031	.0029	.0026	.0024	.0022	.0020
20 years	.0024	.0022	.0019	.0017	.0015	.0013	.0011	.0010

Even if you are almost ready to retire, you should keep your retirement money in moderate-to-higher-risk investments. Why? They have the most growth over time, and your retirement is likely to be long. Given rising longevity and the large number of people who hope to retire relatively early—say between fifty-five and sixty years old—the typical American can expect to live for twenty to forty years after leaving the workaday world. That means your retirement dollars are still invested for the long haul.

The typical rule of thumb for how much of your retirement money you should invest in stocks versus bonds is this: Subtract your age from 100. The result is the percentage of your retirement assets that ought to be in stocks. But it should never be more than 80 percent or less than 20 percent—or so says the rule of thumb. You can better determine what percentages you're comfortable with by reading about risk in Chapter 2.

Goal: Regular Income

CHANCES ARE if you're looking for regular income from your savings, you've passed the accumulation phase of your life and are in the spending phase. In other words, you're probably retired and living on your savings. You don't need to calculate an amount to save. You need good ideas about which investments you ought to consider to derive a decent amount of regular income from your nest egg. The appropriate investments for you will be listed primarily in the "Investing for Income" section of Chapter 4 and in Chapter 7, on bonds. However, be sure to put a bit of your money in stocks, too. That helps diversify your holdings, which both increases the stability of your portfolio and provides some potential for growth.

chapter 4

Diversification

G RETA THOUGHT she was following sound financial practice by spreading her investments among more than a dozen mutual funds. She reasoned that her portfolio would be diversified enough to reduce the risk of loss. But when the value of small-company stocks plunged one summer, so did Greta's entire portfolio. It turned out that most of her mutual funds were invested in small-company stocks. The moral of this story: Having a lot of investments does not necessarily make your portfolio diversified. What matters is whether you have a lot of different types of investments.

"It is important to look at the structure of your portfolio and the types of companies that are in it," says Patricia Johnson, vice president at Salomon Smith Barney, Inc. "If you are buying all pharmaceutical stocks or all technology stocks or all international stocks, you are not diversifying," no matter how many different company or mutual fund shares you buy.

The purpose of diversification is to protect your overall portfolio from major shocks. Because different types of investments tend to move at different times—one investment may be moving up in value when another is moving down—having a variety of investments lends stability to a portfolio.

Diversification, however, can also reduce your overall return, as does any strategy that reduces risk. (But you already know that, because you read Chapter 2.) Consider: A portfolio of big-company stocks gained about 11.2 percent annually on average since 1926, whereas a portfolio that is half stocks and half government bonds returned 8.5 percent. In terms of total wealth over a long time, that difference is substantial. Invest $10,000 at 8.5 percent and leave it alone for thirty years, and you'll have $126,924. Invest the same amount at 11.2 percent, and you'll have more than twice as much: $283,440, to be exact.

So the real trick to diversification is doing just enough to allow yourself to sleep—and meet near-term goals—without doing so much that you rob yourself of generous long-term returns.

How do you do it? If you have read Chapter 3 and followed the instructions, you've already taken the first step, which is to divide your investments by goal. That allows you to allocate your assets based on just how long you have before you need that specific pile of cash—and just how you'd react if the pile was a bit bigger or smaller than you'd planned. That determination immediately leads you toward different investment categories, because the nature of various investments makes them best suited for specific purposes. As you go along, you'll see more clearly why.

Your second step is to diversify your holdings within asset categories. So, for instance, you've already figured out that you need

X amount of money for retirement and that the bulk of that money ought to be invested in the growth investment category. However, you now realize there are a wide array of different growth investments to choose from. You've got to pick one, two, or several to diversify your portfolio within that asset group. That should prevent your entire retirement fund from evaporating before you spend it.

If you have dedicated a lot of money to a specific category, you'll want to choose several investments within it or invest through a mutual fund, which will do that for you. If your pot of cash in a particular category is small, you can make do with just one or two investments per category.

What are your choices?

Investing for Safety

THE PRIMARY CHARACTERISTIC OF SUPERSAFE INVESTMENTS—CALLED "CASH AND CASH EQUIVALENTS" BY those in the know on Wall Street—is that they have some type of government backing that protects the principal. They're highly liquid, which means you can get your hands on your money fairly quickly and easily. That makes all of these investments ideal places to put your emergency money.

The downside: because there is so little risk, there's virtually no return. Once you factor in inflation and income taxes, you can expect to actually lose buying power over time in each of these investments. As a result, you want to be careful not to put more money in safe, low-yielding investments than absolutely necessary.

If you completed the Emergency Money section in Chapter 3 and came out with a big number to be invested in this category—an amount exceeding three to six months' wages—you might want to recheck your figures while reminding yourself that you're saving for fairly likely emergencies only. Remember, too, that unused borrowing power on your credit cards can be used just like an emergency fund. If you've got credit cards that you're not using, you can use them to pay for your auto repairs and even medical bills, if you're in a pinch. Naturally, you'll want to pay off the credit cards as quickly as possible after your emergency has passed—credit card debt is expensive. But they can provide you with a little extra leeway.

Enough said. Here are your choices when you're investing for safety:

Bank Deposits

WHETHER YOUR MONEY is in a checking account, passbook savings account, money market account, or short-term certificate of deposit, deposits in your local bank or savings and loan have the dual advantage of being available at nearly a moment's notice and being federally insured up to $100,000.

What will this money earn? It depends on the type of account and market conditions when you're depositing. However, checking accounts typically pay just 1 percent to 3 percent, depending on your balance. On the bright side, banks normally waive your monthly checking account fees if you maintain a minimum balance—usually anywhere from $500 to $1,500. That can save you anywhere from $3 to $10 a month. Since you need a checking account to pay your bills, maintaining that minimum balance gives you some cushion and saves you a fee, which isn't half bad.

Passbook savings accounts frequently earn no more than your checking account, and they're half as useful. On occasion they'll pay 1 percent or 2 percent more than the checking account, but once you consider the fact that they don't (usually) land you free checking, that's no big bargain. But every bank is a little different, so check to see if your bank aggregates all your balances when determining whether to waive your checking account fees.

If it does, and the passbook account pays more, certainly take advantage of it.

Money market accounts at banks are almost the same as passbook savings, except the bank gives you a checkbook to go with the account. But chances are, the bank won't let you write small checks on the account without some sort of penalty.

Certificates of deposit, more commonly called CDs, are deposit contracts between you and the bank. You agree to deposit your money for a set period of time; the bank agrees to pay you a set rate of interest over that same time period. If you pull your money out before the time is up, you get penalized. (Usually the bank takes away all or part of the interest you earned.) The rate on your CD varies with the duration and size of the deposit. Short-term CDs usually pay less than long-term CDs. Big depositors are offered better rates than small depositors are.

A short-term CD is a great place to put money for predictable short-term goals. For instance, if you need to have $500 or $1,000 saved to pay your next insurance premium or your real estate taxes, you can plunk that money into a CD. Since you know when those payments are due, you can choose a CD that matures at just the right time. By the same token, because you've locked your money up for a set period (taken a little risk), the bank is likely to pay you a bit more than it would pay on a passbook savings or money market account.

Money Market Mutual Funds

MONEY MARKET MUTUAL FUNDS are offered by mutual fund companies (see Chapter 8) rather than banks. While they are considered very safe, because they invest in short-term government and corporate securities and bank deposits, they do not guarantee your principal value. As a result, they pay somewhat higher average rates of return—usually about 2 or 3 percentage points more than a bank money market account (which does offer a guarantee of your principal value). Usually you have the ability to write checks against these accounts, but the mutual fund company may limit the number of checks you can write each year, so generally speaking, these cannot be used to pay your monthly bills. However, they can be used, like CDs, to hold money for big near-term obligations, such as insurance and tax payments.

Unless your fund manager is doing something fancy (and probably unadvisable), you should expect these funds to pay roughly the same amount as you'd get if you invested in a mixture of short-term Treasury securities (see below) and bank deposits. If your fund is paying considerably more, carefully read the prospectus (see Chapter 8). Particularly concentrate on the section in the prospectus labeled "risks." If you are getting a higher return, you are taking a bigger risk. There's no way around it. That's OK as long as you know what the risks are and you're prepared to handle them.

Short-Term Treasury Securities

EVERY WEEK the U.S. government borrows money by issuing short-term IOUs that pay set rates of interest. These IOUs are called Treasury bills, and they are held by literally millions of investors all around the globe.

Treasury bills technically don't pay interest. Instead, they're sold at a discount to their face value. In other words, a $10,000 fifty-two-week bill may sell for $9,500. At maturity, the buyer gets back the $10,000 face value—$500 more than was paid—which generates an effective yield of 5.26 percent.

You can buy Treasury bills that mature—or pay off—in thirteen weeks, twenty-six weeks, or fifty-two weeks. They are sold in minimum denominations of $10,000. If you have more than $10,000 to invest, you can buy additional bills in multiples of $1,000.

Treasury bills can be purchased through a broker or directly from the Treasury. If you buy them from a broker, you will pay a commission that simply reduces the rate of return that you'll earn on each T-bill. If you buy them from the Treasury, you don't pay a commission, but you'll have to set up an account with the Treasury department to get started, which is a touch less convenient.

Treasuries, like bank deposits, are backed by the full faith and credit of the U.S. government. That makes them very safe and secure. However, if you try to sell one before it matures, you might get slightly less than its face value. Treasury yields vary based on interest rates at the time they're sold. Their average return since 1926 has been 3.77 percent, according to Ibbotson Associates, a Chicago-based market research and consulting firm.

Investing for Income

A T SOME POINT IN YOUR LIFE—PERHAPS AFTER YOU RETIRE, PERHAPS SOONER—YOU'LL WANT AT LEAST A portion of your investments to generate income. That income can be used to supplement your wages, Social Security benefits, or pension, making your life more comfortable. Even before you want income to live on, however, you might want to include some income-oriented investments in your portfolio to handle shorter-term and medium-term goals that are important to you—things like buying a house or car or paying your teenager's college tuition. There are numerous investments that can provide that income, including bank certificates of deposit, bonds, and dividend-paying stocks.

Didn't we talk about CDs in the "safety" investing category? And aren't stocks listed under "growth investing"? Yes. But the CDs and stocks mentioned here are significantly different from those discussed above. That's because the CDs purchased for income are the longer-term variety, which will pay higher rates of interest in exchange for your promise to leave your principal alone for a significant time. If you break your promise, you'll pay for it—sometimes dearly.

Meanwhile, although many growth stocks pay dividends, those dividends usually account for just a tiny fraction of the total return on a growth stock investment. On the other hand, some "mature" companies have reached a point where they are unlikely to grow quickly, if at all. At that stage, instead of plowing profits back into the business to help it grow, these companies pay out a large portion of their profits to investors in the form of quarterly cash dividends. These companies are considered "income" stocks. Many of these same companies also issue so-called preferred stocks, which, despite the name, bear a far greater resemblance to bonds than to stocks.

What are the risks and rewards of the different income-oriented investments?

Certificates of Deposit

CERTIFICATES OF DEPOSIT are bank deposits, like any other. They're insured by the federal government to $100,000, which means you can't lose any principal—and usually can't lose any of the promised interest—unless you pull your money out of the bank before the end of the contracted period. (Or unless the principal and interest you have in one institution exceeds $100,000 when the bank fails.)

If you pull your money out early, you are likely to face an early withdrawal penalty that can amount to six months of interest payments or more. If your savings have not generated enough interest to pay the penalty, the bank has the right to take the penalty out of your principal.

How much would the early withdrawal penalty be on your CD? It varies based on the maturity and the bank. On a six-month CD, it's common to be charged one month's interest. On a five-year CD, the penalty can be between six months' and one year's worth of interest. If there's any chance that you'll need your funds before the end of the contracted period, ask your banker about the early withdrawal penalties and under what circumstances these penalties can be waived.

Treasury Notes

TREASURY NOTES are a lot like Treasury bills—they're issued and backed by the U.S. government. That government backing means that Uncle Sam promises to pay back the principal and interest on your note, as long as you hold the note to maturity.

The difference between Treasury notes and Treasury bills is how long they take to mature, or pay back your principal. Whereas Treasury bills are short-term investments, with maturities of one year or less, Treasury notes can be purchased with two-year, three-year, five-year, or ten-year maturities. Remember that the government pays back your principal on the maturity date, but it generally sends you interest payments at regular intervals during the years that you hold the note.

However, Treasury notes are often sold before maturity. If you sell the note before maturity, you could make money or lose money on the sale. Generally speaking, when interest rates fall, the market value of old high-interest notes rises (because you have an investment that guarantees a higher rate of return than the market currently offers). Conversely, when market interest rates rise, the value of old, relatively low-interest notes falls.

Treasury notes are sold in denominations of $1,000 or more. They can be purchased directly from the government through the Treasury's noncompetitive bidding process, or they can be purchased through brokers. Under normal circumstances, Treasury notes pay higher interest rates than Treasury bills.

Treasury Bonds

THESE ARE THE SAME as Treasury notes, but they're issued with even longer maturities. You can buy Treasury bonds that mature thirty or forty years from the date they are issued. Again, as long as you hold the bonds to maturity, the U.S. government promises to pay back your principal, plus interest at a set rate. Similarly, if you sell before maturity, the amount of money you make or lose is based on the prevailing interest rates and market conditions at the time of the sale.

It's important to note that while the value of Treasury notes varies somewhat when interest rates climb or fall, the value of Treasury bonds varies much more. That's simply because your money is locked up at a set interest rate for a longer period of time. That makes Treasury bonds more volatile than the shorter-term Treasury notes and far more volatile than the very short-term Treasury bills.

However, since volatility is a type of risk, and you usually get rewarded for taking increased risks in the financial markets, Treasury bonds typically pay more—often 1 or 2 percentage points more—than ten-year Treasury notes. (You'll find more on bonds in Chapter 7.)

Ginnie Maes

THESE ARE THE BEST KNOWN of a variety of so-called mortgage-backed securities. What's a mortgage-backed security? It's a loan that's pooled together with a bunch of other loans and then turned into a security through the magic of investment banking.

Let's look at an example to explain how they work: John and Jane Doe buy a house and finance it with a $100,000, 9 percent fixed-rate loan. Their bank then sells the Does' mortgage to a third party. It may be to another bank or financial institution, but usually it is to one of several quasi-governmental agencies such as the Government National Mortgage Association (Ginnie Mae), the Federal National Mortgage Association (Fannie Mae), or the Federal Home Loan Mortgage Corporation (Freddie Mac).

Despite their cutesy names, Ginnie, Freddie, and Fannie are major corporations with some U.S. government backing. They take the Does' mortgage and put it into a pool of similar mortgages that pay like amounts of interest and are expected to pay off at the same time. They then sell interests in this pool of mortgages to investors. What investors get when they buy a Ginnie Mae, for instance, is a bond that pays somewhat less than what the Does are paying on their loan. (If the Does pay 9 percent, for example, the investors may get 8 percent; the 1 percent difference is eaten up in fees and charges.) Because Ginnie, Fannie, and Freddie are government backed, these organizations must make up for any losses if the Does stop paying on their loan.

There's only one problem with the securities sold by Ginnie, Freddie, and Fannie: the Does. John and Jane may never default on their loan, but when interest rates fall, they are going to refinance their mortgage to get a lower rate. So instead of getting comparatively high rates of interest for thirty years, investors in mortgage-backed securities are likely to get back only their principal. In marketspeak, that's called prepayment risk. If rates rise, the Does will hang on to their mortgage, and investors will be stuck with comparatively low-yielding securities for thirty years. That's called interest-rate risk.

CMOs

COLLATERALIZED MORTGAGE OBLIGATIONS, or CMOs, started life as mortgage-backed securities. But then some smart investment bankers thought about the problem with the Does. They knew they couldn't change the Does' behavior, but they could find ways to "restructure" the average mortgage-backed security to shift around some of the prepayment risk and interest-rate risk.

How? They took the Does' mortgage (and thousands of other

mortgages like it) and sliced it into pieces. Each piece included an element of the original mortgage. For instance, one slice might give investors the right to half of the interest payments made by the Does, plus the first repayment of principal. The next piece might give the investor the right to the second repayment of principal, plus another half of the interest. A final piece might be structured like a zero-coupon bond, where the investor doesn't get anything until the bond matures, at which time he's repaid an amount that works out to what he paid for the bond plus some. (In reality, CMOs are usually cut into more slices than that, but you get the idea.)

Of course, investors who buy the first type of CMO have the greatest prepayment risk, while investors in the final category have the greatest interest-rate risk. Investment bankers assess the risks of each slice (or "tranch," as they like to say on Wall Street), and they price the securities with that in mind. Thus, some CMOs—which usually sell in minimum denominations ranging from $1,000 to $25,000—sell for less than their face value, whereas others sell for more.

Corporate Bonds

SOME COMPANIES finance growth by selling debt—IOUs—to investors. These formal IOUs are called bonds, and in many ways, they're like the bonds issued by the U.S. Treasury. They have stated interest rates and maturity dates, and they're sold through brokers. However, because individual companies are presumably less financially secure than the U.S. government, which can exercise its taxing authority if it ever runs short of cash, corporations typically pay higher rates of interest than the U.S. Treasury pays on bonds with similar maturity dates.

The less financially secure the corporation, the higher the interest rate. You're taking a bigger risk that the company will default and fail to pay back your principal and interest, so you get a higher return. When the bonds are especially high risk and high yield, they're called junk bonds.

Conversely, bonds issued by healthy companies—or backed by bond insurance—pay comparatively less interest but pose far less default risk to investors. High-quality bonds are frequently termed investment quality, triple-A, double-A, or simply A-rated bonds.

Properly chosen, this type of bond can increase the yield on the income portion of your investment portfolio while only modestly increasing the risks.

Municipal Bonds

ISSUED BY state and local governments and some government agencies, municipal bonds pay relatively low interest rates, but the interest you earn is usually federal and state tax free. That can make these bonds attractive to investors who are in high tax brackets and who would otherwise have to pay a large portion of their interest earnings to Uncle Sam (and, perhaps, to Aunt California or Aunt New York).

Like corporate bonds, municipal bonds are graded. Some are good quality, some poor. Some are backed by private insurance companies that promise to pay bondholders the principal and interest that's due if the issuer fails to pay. By and large, the safer your municipal bond, the less interest you get.

REITs

REAL ESTATE INVESTMENT TRUSTS, or REITs, are publicly traded investment companies that pour their cash into shopping centers, medical buildings, and mortgages on commercial properties. They resemble closed-end mutual funds (see Chapter 8). After they are launched through a public offering, their shares usually trade on major U.S. stock exchanges and are sold through stockbrokers. The shares can sell at a discount or a premium to the company's net asset value.

On the bright side, REITs distribute 95 percent of their taxable earnings to investors each year. These earnings come from two sources: rents on the real estate owned by the REIT and capital gains from selling real estate. Consequently, as an investor, you are exposed to two risks: a rotten real estate market, where property values decline; and/or a rotten rental market, where there is more rental space than renters.

As a practical matter, it's tough to find a REIT that isn't going to suffer from one of these risks eventually. That's simply because the moment a rental real estate market gets hot—a lot of prospective tenants move in—developers rush to meet the demand by creating more office space. Rental markets go through regular shortage/glut cycles. The result: In good years, a REIT's taxable earnings can be substantial—anywhere from 8 percent to around 20 percent. In bad years, REITs can lose equal amounts and pay virtually nothing to investors.

Indeed, even in good markets, you have to be very careful about what REIT you buy. Some have been plagued by questionable insider deals that have drastically increased management costs, reduced share value, and eliminated dividend payouts to investors.

Want to know more? The National Association of Real Estate Investment Trusts hosts a great Web site (www.nareit.com) that includes helpful articles and details about different types of REITs. However, if you choose to invest, make sure you take a long and careful look at the industry's historical returns first. These investments are exceptionally volatile.

Preferred Stocks

THIS INVESTMENT CLASS used to describe stocks in the true sense of the word. However, in 1993, most of these securities were restructured for tax reasons. (The reasons are complex and mostly boring, but the bottom line is that issuers can get a tax deduction for paying interest but not for paying dividends, so they restructured preferred stocks to resemble bonds rather than dividend-paying stocks.) Technically how "preferreds" work is this: A company sells long-term bonds to a trust, which then issues preferred shares that pass on the bond interest to investors.

Since the new preferreds are geared to individual investors, they are sold in bite-sized denominations. They generally are sold at $25 per share at initial issue. Most are listed on the New York Stock Exchange, so they can be bought and sold freely.

Their value, like the value of the underlying bonds, is affected by interest rates. When rates rise, the value of preferred shares can fall sharply. When rates fall, the value of preferred shares rises, but fairly modestly.

Why do you get less on the upside than the down? Because the bonds that back preferred shares generally have thirty- to forty-year maturities. But they also have so-called call dates at five- or ten-year intervals. In other words, the issuer can choose to buy back your debt by paying par value—$25—for your shares on the call date. The issuer is not obligated to buy back or redeem your shares. It simply has the right to do so. As a result, issuers redeem preferred shares on the call date when interest rates have fallen since the time of issue. That allows them to refinance their debt at lower rates of interest. That means you don't get to lock in that preferential interest rate for very long.

On the other hand, if interest rates are rising, the issuers are not going to redeem their bonds. You are saddled with a relatively low-yielding investment for the duration—unless you want to sell your shares on the open market. And if you do, you should expect to sell for less than the $25 face value. On the bright side, preferred stocks tend to pay interest a little more frequently than bonds. Bonds usually pay interest every six months; preferred stocks normally pay interest every three months.

Because of the higher prepayment and interest-rate risk that you take when buying preferreds, you also should expect a somewhat higher yield than you'd get on an ordinary bond. Typically, preferreds pay about 1.5 to 2 percentage points more than comparable Treasury bonds and 0.25 to 0.5 percentage points more than comparable corporate bonds.

Income Stocks

WHAT KIND OF COMPANY would accept growth prospects that are so lackluster that the company simply gives most of its income away to shareholders? Traditionally, utilities.

Utility companies are regulated and often restricted to doing business in a set geographic area. They sell a commodity—such as water, electric power, or gas—that is not likely to see a big upsurge or drop in demand. (Your need and desire for water is dictated by thirst and landscaping. Unless there's dramatic growth in a community—lots of thirsty people move there and plant lawns—the community's demand for water doesn't change much from year to year. And a community's growth is limited by the available amount of real estate.) So when a utility completes its expansion—has the majority of its power plants built and its infrastructure solid—it becomes a cash cow for investors. Dividend yields at utility companies often can range from 5 percent to 8 percent.

What's a dividend yield? It's a ratio that indicates how much money the company pays out in annual dividends compared to what you originally paid for the stock. Let's say, for example, that you bought 100 shares of a company for $10 a share, and that company pays dividends of $.15 per share each quarter, or $.60 per share each year. Your $1,000 investment pays $60 annually. That's a 6 percent dividend yield, because $60 divided by $1,000 is 0.06, or 6 percent.

The benefit of income stocks is that you get current income and you get the chance to participate in the company's stock price appreciation, if the company happens to have a good year that's reflected in its stock price. The bad side is you also would participate in the company's stock price depreciation, if the company had an unusually bad year. Worse still, there's no law requiring a company to continue paying regular cash dividends. If the company decides it can no longer afford to pay you that $60 annually, it can unilaterally announce that the dividends will stop, and there's little, if anything, you can do about it.

Investing for Growth

I F THERE'S SOMETHING BIG THAT YOU WANT—FROM A COMFORTABLE RETIREMENT TO A MANSION ON THE beach—and you can't afford it today, you need to save and make your money work for you. When you have lots of time, the best way to do that is to invest for growth.

There are two main investments in this category: domestic stocks and international stocks. Both are volatile, which is another way of saying they're likely to experience wide swings in value. However, over long periods of time, there's good reason to believe stocks also will appreciate dramatically faster than any other type of asset. That makes it easier to attain your long-term goals.

Here's the rundown on how domestic and international stock markets work, as well as their risks and rewards.

Domestic Stocks

WHEN YOU BUY a share of stock, you are buying a piece of the issuing company. Admittedly, it's probably a small piece, but that share you purchased gives you the right to participate in the company's wealth (or fiscal decline) and vote on matters of some importance—directors, company auditors, and some shifts in corporate policy.

In some cases, you are also entitled to dividends—payments of cash or stock to shareholders. Some companies also provide their shareholders with perquisites, such as tickets to the company's theme parks or discounts on its merchandise.

Because companies tend to grow and prosper over time—and

71

because a share of stock allows you to participate in the prosperity—stock prices, in the aggregate, tend to appreciate over long periods of time. However, individually, some companies prosper; others fail. If you buy a share in a loser, you could lose all, or a significant portion, of your initial investment. In other words, when you invest in stocks, you risk losing your initial investment, but because you are taking a bigger risk, you get the opportunity to earn far bigger rewards.

How big a reward? The Chicago-based research company Ibbotson Associates has tracked the performance of U.S. stocks from 1926 to the present. That period includes the Great Depression, the New Deal, World War II, the Korean conflict, the Vietnam War, the Kennedy assassination, Reaganomics, and the Gulf War, not to mention the lunar landing, the breakup of Ma Bell, the Watergate scandal, and the dismantling of the Iron Curtain.

In other words, it is a fairly diverse period that has had its share of ups and downs, just like any period in history. During that time, the average annual return on small-company U.S. stocks was about 12.4 percent. The average annual return on big-company stocks was 11.2 percent. Over the same period, inflation rose 3.1 percent per year, and the return on U.S. Treasury bills was 3.77 percent.

To put it another way: If you had a diversified portfolio of large-company stocks during that period, the value of your investment portfolio rose 8.1 percentage points faster than the rate of inflation. For every $100 you put in the market, you hiked your buying power by $8.10 each year. At the end of twenty years, your real (inflation-adjusted) buying power increased fivefold, to $503 from $100, without any additional payments from you.

Although investing is as much an art as a science, it's reasonable to expect that future investment returns will mirror historic returns over long periods. In other words, it's reasonable to assume that stocks will continue to appreciate faster than the rate of inflation and other types of traditional investments.

The downside: it is also reasonable to assume that stocks could repeat their short-term historic performance over shorter periods, too. And that's been far less illustrious than the long-term performance. To be specific: the market crash of 1929 so depressed stock prices that investors who put $100 in the market then saw the value of their securities fall to less than $20 at the market's nadir in 1932. It took roughly eight years before securities prices rose back to ground zero, where $100 invested in 1929 was worth $100 again. And then the market took another sickening slide, from which it didn't recover until after World War II had ended. From start to finish, it was a full fifteen years of pain for stock market investors.

The market also took a sharp, decade long dive in 1969. And it experienced short-term "crashes" in 1987, 1989, and 1990. But its performance in 1995 was enough to make an investor beam. Stock values as measured by the Standard and Poor's 500 index were up more than 37 percent. The years following have been almost as impressive. Big-company stocks posted a 23 percent gain in 1996, a 33 percent gain in 1997, a 28 percent gain in 1998, and a 21 percent gain in 1999.

Incidentally, although investors in small companies have done better than investors in large companies over the long haul (average annual returns of 12.4 percent versus 11.2 percent, respectively), at various points in time, small-company stocks do worse than big-company stocks. They fall farther and faster, and they stay depressed longer.

These heady climbs and sickening slumps are called volatility. When an investment is as volatile as the stock market, it is unwise to invest unless you have a fairly long time horizon that allows you to wait out the price swings and go for the long-term price appreciation.

How long is a "fairly long" time horizon? That depends on you and why you are investing. Let's say you want to buy a house in five years, and you're trying to determine where to invest the down-payment money. The stock market would be a good place for all or part of that money if you wouldn't be crushed if your home-buying plans had to be put off because of a market slump that depressed the value of your investment portfolio and thus reduced the amount you had saved for the down payment. What if you would be crushed if you couldn't buy the home as planned? Then put the down payment money in bonds that mature (or pay back their principal) at the same time as your plans do.

Stocks are also ideal to have in your retirement portfolio. The younger and farther from retirement you are, the more stocks you can handle. And they're a good choice for college funds for young children. However, if you are investing in individual stocks rather than mutual funds, you must diversify your portfolio by buying stocks in several different companies that do business in several different industries. That ensures that your net worth won't crash if one industry, whether it's oil, technology, or retailing, hits a slump. Experts suggest you own shares in at least eight to ten different companies. Ideally, those companies should be operating in substantially different industries.

Foreign Stocks

JUST AS U.S. COMPANIES issue ownership interests in the form of stock, so do foreign companies. The risks and rewards of foreign stock markets are similar to those of the U.S. stock market, but they frequently are magnified. There are a variety of reasons why, including political instability in some countries and the fact that many foreign markets are smaller and more thinly traded than the U.S. market. That tends to make them subject to wider price swings, both up and down.

In addition, U.S. investors who buy foreign equities face something called currency risk. Here's why. When you buy stock in a foreign country, you buy the shares with that country's currency. When you sell them, you get paid in that country's currency, too. Before you can spend the proceeds in the United States, you have to convert the foreign currency into U.S. dollars at the going exchange rate. And exchange rates vary day to day based on the relative strength of any given country's balance sheet and the interest rates that country is paying on government securities (the equivalent of Treasury bills). If currency values in the foreign land have risen since you purchased your foreign stocks, you win when you exchange the currency. If they fall, however, you lose.

In some cases, the currency swings can be more significant to your total return than the actual appreciation or depreciation of the particular stocks you purchased (see Chapter 10). On the bright side, there are years when a foreign country's stock market can nearly double in value. And if currency swings are working in your favor at the same time, your returns can be stunning.

Equity Mutual Funds

MUTUAL FUNDS are investment companies that pool the money of many investors and buy securities in bulk. The securities that a fund buys are determined by the fund's investment objectives. These investment objectives are spelled out in the prospectus and by the fund manager, who makes the investment decisions.

So-called equity funds—also known as growth or aggressive growth funds—buy stock in U.S. companies. When you buy a share in an equity fund, you're actually buying an interest in all of the different stocks held by that fund. That gives you the benefit of broad diversification, which reduces the risk that your investment portfolio will be savaged by a single bad stock. In essence, if you buy the right mutual fund, you may not need to diversify the stock portion of your portfolio further. One fund could do it all.

There are lots of other benefits and tricks to buying mutual funds. However, since an entire chapter is devoted to investing in them (Chapter 8), let it suffice to say that investing in equity mutual funds is an alternative to investing in individual stocks. It is a particularly good alternative for those who don't want to spend a lot of time picking individual investments or for those who are starting out and don't have a lot of money.

Global/International Mutual Funds

JUST AS BUYING SHARES in a domestic equity mutual fund is similar to buying domestic stocks, buying shares in global and international mutual funds is similar to buying shares in foreign stocks.

The big benefit to buying foreign stocks through a fund is that global mutual funds not only spread your money among numerous stocks, they also can spread the investments among numerous countries. That reduces currency risk, too. Moreover, because of language barriers and steep trading costs involved in buying and selling individual foreign shares, global and international mutual funds may well be the smartest way to get a little international flavor in your portfolio. We'll talk more about that in Chapter10.

Investments that Protect You from Inflation

FOR SOME PEOPLE, THE GOAL OF INVESTING IS NOT SO MUCH GETTING AHEAD AS IT IS NOT FALLING BEHIND. Because inflation marches forward each and every year, the fear is that you will fall behind if your investments don't rise as quickly as the cost of buying necessary goods and services.

There is also a group of investors who fear that the U.S. dollar could become worthless someday. At that point, the only way to buy things you need would be to trade "hard assets," such as precious metals and gems, or barter something you have, like food, for something they have, like shelter. (Personally, I figure if things get this bad, your investment portfolio will be the least of your worries, but. . .)

Three types of investments are widely considered inflation hedges: precious metals, real estate, and a relatively new type of Treasury bonds called real-return bonds.

Precious Metals

IF YOU TALK TO A GOLD BUG, he'll tell you that gold—the bell-wether of precious-metal investments—holds its value over time. An ounce of gold would buy you a suit of clothes in the days of Henry VIII, and it will still buy you a suit of clothes today.

What gold bugs won't tell you is that while inflation has risen 3.1 percent per year since 1925, the value of gold—which became publicly traded in the United States in the late 1970s—has fallen from about $800 per ounce in 1980 to less than $300 today. In other words, whereas it would buy you a marvelous suit and plenty of accessories in 1980, it would buy you a merely adequate suit and, perhaps, an inexpensive pair of socks in 1999.

There are other disadvantages to buying gold, too. Namely, if you buy gold bullion or coins, you have to store them some-where—like in a bank safe deposit box. And a safe deposit box is likely to cost you $40 to $60 a year. In addition, gold doesn't pay dividends and it doesn't pay interest. It just sits there. In a box. In the bank. In the dark.

It's tough to justify buying bullion with a reasonable argument that doesn't include some kind of doomsday scenario. (Although the U.S. may suffer economic ills in the future, many safeguards have been placed into the economic system since the 1930s, rang-ing from Social Security to unemployment insurance and Federal Deposit Insurance. These safeguards make it unlikely that the nation will suffer economic disasters as severe as the Great Depression in the future.) However, there have been times when you could make a small fortune merely by speculating in the gold market by buying shares in gold-mining companies. When infla-tion fears are high, for example, the value of gold tends to rise.

When per-ounce prices rise a nudge, the value of gold-mining shares often soars. If you are quick on your feet—or on the phone, calling your broker—you can make a tidy sum. But this is less protecting yourself from inflation than it is speculating—rolling the dice and hoping you'll hit seven.

Residential Real Estate

RESIDENTIAL REAL ESTATE—in other words, your home—can provide a real hedge against inflation no matter what happens to the price of your house in the future. How so? By buying a home that you can live in, you eliminate the need to pay rent. That protects you from possible rental rate increases that could come down the road. You also get some tax benefits when you buy residential real estate, so your actual out-of-pocket cost, or after-tax cost, may be less than the sum of your down payment and total monthly payments. (Mortgage interest expenses are tax deductible.)

In addition, if you finance your house with a thirty-year, fixed-rate mortgage, you have ensured that your second-largest household expense (after income taxes) will not budge. Indeed, your personal inflation rate will actually drop at the end of thirty years, because you will have paid off the loan. Then you will be sitting on an asset of substantial value that you can sell, if need be, or simply live in for the rest of your life.

Can you analyze your home as an investment, like you analyze stocks or bonds? Not really. National statistics tracking the price of residential real estate are dubious because they track only sales prices without attempting to determine the size and quality of the residences sold in any given period. (In fact, while the "average" home sales price has risen, so has the average square footage and the average number of bathrooms.) However, real estate prices do appear to rise over long periods of time, seemingly somewhat faster than the rate of inflation.

House prices don't rise in lockstep with inflation. In fact, when inflation is high, real estate prices are likely to fall (because when inflation is high interest rates go up, and when interest rates go up so do mortgage rates, which means people can't afford as much). But later, home prices catch up by taking dramatic leaps in value when inflation and interest rates drop.

If you're a subscriber to the doomsday theory—the idea that inflation will be so high that U.S. currency will become worthless and we'll be driven to barter to survive—you should remember that you can't eat gold, but you can grow vegetables in your backyard.

Real-Return Bonds

REAL-RETURN BONDS, also known as inflation-adjusted bonds, were developed in 1997, with the idea that investors might want an inflation hedge that really did move in lockstep with inflation. These new bonds are pegged to the Consumer Price Index, the main measuring stick of inflation in the United States. They pay a current return, and once a year the bond's principal value is adjusted to reflect hikes in the index. Your future interest payments are then based on the boosted principal value. For example, let's say you bought a $1,000 bond. You earned $35, or 3.5 percent, on it. At the end of the year, the CPI indicates that inflation rose 4 percent that year. The principal value of your bond rises to $1,040. The following year, your interest payments will rise to reflect a 3.5 percent return on a $1,040 principal value. The catch: if your bonds are not in a tax-favored retirement account, both the interest and the inflation adjustment are taxable. So you pay income tax on both the interest and the $40 boost to your principal value, even though you didn't receive the $40 in cash.

Some bond experts are big fans of real-return bonds. The biggest buyers of them to date have been institutions, including mutual funds. So if you are interested in addressing inflation directly but you don't want to buy the bonds yourself, look for so-called income funds that include them in their portfolios.

Speculation

T HERE ARE A WIDE NUMBER OF SPECULATIVE INVEST-
MENTS THAT RANGE FROM LIMITED PARTNERSHIPS TO
commodities contracts to derivative securities. And there are trading strategies, such as buying and selling "puts" and "calls" (stock
options), that can occasionally supercharge—or decimate—the
value of your investment portfolio.

Unless you are both wealthy and highly sophisticated about
investing, you should avoid this type of speculation. Not only is
there a good chance that you will lose all or a significant part of
your money, in some cases you can actually lose more than you
originally invested.

Since this book is for beginning investors, speculative investments are not covered in detail, with one exception: viatical settlements. Why make the exception? Because viatical settlements
are being heavily marketed to unsophisticated investors as a
"safe" and/or "guaranteed" investment that pays double-digit
returns. This is a lie. Viatical settlements are highly speculative
investments. Worse still, in the past several years, the industry has
become pockmarked with swindlers. But to thoroughly understand the risk requires some background both on the industry and
on how these investments work.

Viatical Settlements

THESE SO-CALLED investment vehicles are insurance policies
that are sold to investors, who get paid off when the person whose
life is insured dies. Barry Fisher, an attorney in Century City,
California, dubs them "death futures." Ghoulish, you say?

Absolutely, although the industry started for a very practical (and sympathetic) reason: AIDS, or Acquired Immune Deficiency Syndrome. In the beginning of the U.S. AIDS crisis, when the disease was a mystery and there was nothing to treat it, AIDS patients—primarily young, gay men—were getting horribly ill. Seemingly inexplicably, they would be hit with one ailment after the next, causing them to call in sick time and again. So they lost their jobs. They ran through their savings. They found themselves dying and destitute.

Yet many of them had life insurance. In fact, roughly 75 percent of Americans have life insurance, because big companies commonly provide a certain amount of life insurance as a company-paid employee benefit. And if you have had a policy for some time, it generally cannot be canceled unless you fail to pay the premium. For many of these young men this was a horrible irony. They had no dependents—no children who relied on them for financial support—so they really had no need for life insurance for the traditional reason of protecting their wives and children from the financial disaster that the death of a breadwinner can bring. The policyholders could desperately use the cash from that death benefit, but they had to die to get it.

Viatical settlements sprang up to address this need. Terminally ill AIDS patients could sell their policies to an "investor." That investor would be paid back when the policyholder died. Investors would make a return on the policy by buying it at a discount to its death benefit. In other words, a $100,000 policy might be purchased for $70,000. The AIDS patient would get the cash today; the investor would get a $30,000 profit when the policyholder died.

However, medical advances have helped many AIDS patients live much longer than expected. Meanwhile, con artists have jumped into the viatical settlement market, selling policies on fictitious patients. For a variety of reasons, it's often difficult for investors to differentiate a valid viatical settlement from a fraud.

Worse still, securities regulators who normally attempt to protect investors from investment scams have been unsuccessful in their attempts to regulate viatical settlements. Part of the problem is that they're a hybrid—part insurance, part investment. No one knows who has jurisdiction.

If you're still tempted, check out a book called *Viatical Settlements: An Investor's Guide,* by Gloria Grening Wolk, or visit Wolk's Web site at www.viatical-expert.net.

Other Investments to Avoid

Commodities Futures

THE COMMODITIES MARKETS were formed to battle something that economic texts called "the farm problem." In a nutshell, the farm problem was anticipating future supply and demand. Farmers had to plant their crops a year (or in the case of certain crops, such as coffee, avocados, oranges, and apples, many years) before bringing these products to market. With such a long lead time, it was difficult to know whether the market price for their goods would be sufficient to cover their costs. Often it wasn't, which led to scores of farm bankruptcies.

The commodities market aimed to solve this problem by pre-selling shipments of farm products, from cattle to pigs, corn to coffee. Typically the way you do this is to set up a commodity trading account with your friendly neighborhood broker. The broker will set up a margin account for you as part of the deal. Then, let's say you want to buy a $100,000 coffee-bean contract. The brokerage will typically let you put down just 5 percent to 10 percent of that purchase price in cash. The rest is effectively borrowed.

Naturally, you don't want $100,000 worth of coffee beans (unless you have a coffee factory somewhere to process and sell it later, or unless you're really, really thirsty), so you plan to resell the contract before the coffee actually comes to market. If coffee prices rise, you can make a killing because you've paid just, say, $5,000 to purchase a $100,000 contract. If that $100,000 contract rises 10 percent in value, you earn $10,000 on your $5,000 investment—a 200 percent return on your money. But if coffee prices fall, you can be subject to a margin call. That means you'll have to kick more money into the account. In this unhappy scenario, you could lose several times more than your original investment. If you're not a farmer, a coffee manufacturer, or a person who can handle serious investment losses, this is not a good place to play.

Limited Partnerships

LIMITED PARTNERSHIPS became popular in the early 1980s partly as a result of favorable tax legislation that allowed these partnerships to pass tax losses through to wealthy investors. The partnerships of the early 1980s owned real estate, oil and gas deposits, windmills, and a variety of other speculative and often money-losing ventures. When the tax laws changed in 1986, barring limited partners from claiming tax losses that often exceeded their cash investments, limited partnerships went belly-up in droves.

You can still buy limited partnerships today. They continue to invest in speculative ventures, such as oil and gas, windmills, and low-income housing. For some investors, the low-income-housing partnerships still provide substantial tax breaks. However, the risks come on a variety of fronts. One of the most noteworthy is that the general partner usually has control over what is purchased with the partnership's money and how much is paid in fees to everyone from brokers to the general partner himself. If you have a bad general partner who charges excessive fees, you can have a bad investment even if the partnership's underlying assets are great. There is very little a limited partner can do to stop abuses by a general partner.

"Naked" Options

INVESTORS CAN BUY OR SELL options, which are rights to buy or sell a particular security at a set price in the future. There are conservative ways to use stock options, but going "naked"—trading options on stock you don't own—is a good way to lose whatever amount you've invested and occasionally more.

By and large, what you're doing is guessing about the direction of a stock and betting that it will hit a certain mark by a particular point in time. If it does, you make money. If it doesn't, you lose it.

Let's say, for example, you buy an option to buy 100 shares of XYZ Corp. at $100 on April 15, 2001. Because XYX currently sells for $90 per share, your option is cheap—say, $3 per share, or $300 for the contract to buy those 100 shares. If XYZ's stock soars to $150 in the interim, the fact that your option gives you the right to buy those shares at $50 per share under the market price makes that option very valuable indeed. You make a killing of $47 per share, or $4,700 on your $300 investment.

But what happens if XYZ posts poor quarterly profits and declines in value to $80 or languishes at $90? Your option becomes worthless. If the stock price remains low until after your strike date of April 15, the option expires. You lost whatever amount you spent to buy this option in the first place. The even more frustrating thing is you may have called the direction of the stock correctly. XYZ may hit $100 or even $150 in the future. But because options expire on a particular date, you not only have to be right about the stock, you also have to be right about the timing. That's tough.

Conversely, you can sell a so-called naked put. What does that mean? Let's say you think XYZ is a bad company that's selling at a high price. You figure its stock price is going to decline. So you sell another investor the right to buy XYZ shares from you at $100 in the future. The other investor, who thinks XYZ is great and is going to appreciate, pays you $3 a share (or $300) for that right.

Now, let's say you were wrong. XYZ posts terrific profits. Its stock price soars to $150. You must buy the shares at $150 to sell to the option holder at $100. You lose $47 a share—the $150 you paid for each share that you sold at $100, minus the $3 per share you got for the option. Ouch.

Other Investments You Don't Understand

THEY CAN CROP UP on a regular basis. Somebody talks to you about foreign currency markets; derivative securities; insurance premium finance schemes; strips; or any one of dozens of other investments that you find befuddling. The salesman tells you what a great deal they are, but you can't figure out why this investment pays so much more than the traditional investments you're familiar with. Let that be the red flag that tells you to stay away.

There are two reasons you don't want to invest in things you don't understand:

1   You won't know when to sell, since you really didn't understand why you were buying in the first place.
2   You have no idea whether you've got a legitimate investment or a scam, because you don't understand the investment well enough to ask the right questions to find out.

It's one thing to lose money in a legitimate investment when you understood the risks. It's quite another to lose money in an investment scam or in an investment that posed risks you were not prepared to handle.

Con artists prey on people who don't want to admit they're confused. They'll tell you that you'll earn a 20 percent annual return. They'll tell you that all of your friends are investing and you'll be left out if you don't. They'll tell you that this is a one-time offer. If you don't decide now, you'll miss it. They'll tell you your profits are guaranteed.

If you have the sense to ask why they don't just borrow money from the bank to finance this "opportunity," since the profits are guaranteed, they'll counter with "Bankers don't understand this investment." Make your life simple and decide that if a bank's going to turn down a "guaranteed opportunity," you can, too.

Remember your mantra: Will this investment allow you to have the amount of money you need, when you need it? With the investments just mentioned, there is no way to know. So skip them.

If you are wealthy beyond your wildest dreams one day, and then you decide you want to play in the commodities or foreign currency markets, more power to you. Until then, stick with risks you understand and plain-vanilla investments whose returns you can predict.

chapter 5

Picking Individual Stocks

BILLIONAIRE INVESTOR Warren Buffett looks for value when he buys stocks. Peter Lynch, the investment guru who once headed Fidelity's giant Magellan stock fund, seeks companies with strong growth prospects. Both have been wildly successful, showing that stock-picking success can be achieved from different angles. Indeed, there is no one right way to pick stocks.

Knowing the basics of stock picking is a fundamental skill that all serious investors need to have. One relatively basic method, used in variations by many professionals, is to combine the growth and value strategies prescribed by Buffett and Lynch. Look for steadily growing companies that are selling at reasonable prices, suggests Judy Vale, a portfolio manager at Neuberger & Berman in New York.

Looking at Fundamental Indicators of Value

E XCITING AND VOLATILE MARKETS WARRANT A DULL APPROACH TO INVESTING—AN APPROACH THAT INVOLVES asking a lot of questions about the company's fundamental business, then doing a little mathematical analysis, Vale says. So how do you do it?

While there are no hard-and-fast rules, many professional investors screen companies based on a number of factors, including growth in sales and earnings, cash flow, and net profits. They also look at how profits compare with total assets—a ratio better known as return on assets.

These figures are important because the future value of a company's shares is likely to hinge on its ability to grow and prosper. Growth in sales and earnings is a mathematical reading of demand for a company's products and services. Meanwhile, a company that's earning a substantial amount on assets—Vale's standard requires more than a 1 percent return on assets for a financial services concern and more than 8 percent for nonfinancial businesses—has proved it knows how to deploy its resources in effective ways.

In terms of cash flow, look for whether the company is generating more cash from operations than it's spending. That tells you if the company is earning enough on its business to finance future growth without resorting to borrowing or issuing more stock— either of which can prove detrimental to existing shareholders.

Finally, try to determine whether the company has a product or provides a service that's unique and difficult to copy. If it does, it's likely the company will remain a market leader for a longer period of time. What products are hard to copy or unique? There are a wide variety, but they would include products that require formulas that are under patent protection for long periods, those that require unique technical skills, or those that require a great deal of capital to produce—such as cars and airplanes, for example.

If the company makes it through that gauntlet, its stock is analyzed to determine whether the price is cheap or dear. Often that analysis hinges on the price-to-earnings (P/E) ratio, which is a measure of how the company's stock price compares to its per-share earnings. A company that earns $2 per share annually and sells for $20, for example, would have a P/E ratio of 10. This company's stock price is equivalent to ten times its annual earnings per share.

When looking at this ratio, what investors must keep in mind is that there is not one right P/E ratio for all companies. Instead, each company has a normal P/E range. When the company's stock price breaks out of that range, it's time to ask why. If the company's stock price is higher than normal compared with earnings, it can be an indication that its stock price is too high. Or it can indicate that the company is primed for unusually fast growth. Likewise, when a company's P/E is low, it can mean either that bad times are setting in or that the company's stock price is a bargain.

The rule of thumb for considering the price of growth stocks that have broken out of their normal P/E ratio is this: The stock is still a good buy if the P/E is at or below the annual growth rate of the company's earnings. In other words, a stock that normally sold for fifteen times earnings might be a legitimate bargain when selling for twenty times earnings if its profits were growing by 20 percent or 25 percent per year.

Where do you find this average price-to-earnings range and a professional reading on the question of whether the stock is over-priced or cheap? There are numerous sources, but one of the most valuable—and easiest to find—is the *Value Line Investment Survey.* Value Line publishes detailed analyses of about 1,700 publicly traded stocks and ranks them for "timeliness" and volatility. These rankings are updated each week and are available in most major public libraries. (Many institutional investors subscribe to *Value Line*, but the subscription cost—$570 annually for the print survey and $595 annually for the electronic version—is high for a small investor.)

For investors who prefer small-company stocks, Value Line also offers a second book, its *Expanded Survey,* which looks at 1,800 companies that are too small to get into its regular investment survey.

Stocks that receive 1 and 2 timeliness rankings are those that Value Line thinks will end up on the top of the heap over the next six to twelve months. Value Line reports also give a history of the company's P/E and rates its cash flow and growth. The reports don't replace getting an annual report directly from the company, but they can certainly help investors narrow the search.

Take caution about narrowing your stock choices based on Value Line's timeliness rankings: Sometimes the top-ranked companies are all clustered in just a few industries. If you aim to diversify properly—a requisite for anyone who wants to reduce his or her risks—you have to keep an eye on the industry groups you're choosing and make sure you choose stocks in many different industries.

Once you've chosen a stable of stocks to buy, all you need to do is keep an eye on your selections to make sure you didn't select poorly. Doing that periodic analysis will help you determine when you ought to sell—and when it's time to buy more shares in the companies you like the best. There's more on that in Chapter 6.

Reading a Financial Statement

THERE ARE THREE STEPS TO PICKING INDIVIDUAL STOCKS FOR THE LONG TERM. THE FIRST STEP IS FIGURING OUT which industries will benefit from long-term trends, such as the globalization of the financial markets, the aging of the population, and the revolution in technology. The industries you expect to do better than others are ideal places to invest your money. The second step is finding a few—or a few dozen—specific companies in those industries that you want to consider more closely. The third step is the trickiest. That's when you've got to examine each company's finances to cull the likely winners from the losers.

Sound daunting? It's not as bad as it might appear, because most companies will provide you with all of the information you need. You simply need to ask for the appropriate reports and learn which numbers are the most telling.

"People think that they can't do what I do, but the basics are really easy," says Donna Takeda, vice president of securities research and economics at Merrill Lynch & Co. in New York. "All we are doing is looking carefully at public documents. They tell you pretty much everything you need to know."

What You Need

TO START THE PROCESS, get a copy of the company's annual report to shareholders and its 10K filing. You can generally get these by simply requesting them from the company's investor relations office. (You can also read, download, or print this information off the Web. However, if you get the data off the Internet, make sure you are looking at the full financial statement rather than a summary version that might leave out important facts.)

The annual report and 10K are similar documents. Both show how the company has done during the previous year and on a longer-term basis. However, you need both because the annual report doesn't always reveal certain sticky financial details, and the 10K doesn't give you much of the personality of the company and its management.

Yes, companies have personalities, which generally reflect the nature of the company's chief executive officer. Knowing this personality—whether aggressive, innovative, egotistical, or traditional—can help you predict what the company might do in the future.

Generally, you can start by looking at the annual report. It's prettier—usually including photographs and graphics—and generally easier to read than the 10K. However, if you find that it doesn't have several years of financial information and lots of detail, toss it aside and look at the 10K instead.

"They're essentially similar, but the 10K is a more complete document," says Robert Bayless, chief accountant in the Securities and Exchange Commission's corporate finance division. "You'll find more detailed descriptions of the business, allowances for losses, and contracts for significant transactions in the 10K."

Where to Start

FLIP TO THE MIDDLE of the annual report, where you'll find a five- or ten-year comparison of "selected financial data." This chart shows year-to-year sales, operating income, net income, earnings per share, and balance sheet data that include how much the company holds in assets, liabilities, and working capital.

Your first move is to start making comparisons. Divide the current-year revenue, or sales, by the previous-year revenue and subtract one from the result. That gives you the year-to-year growth in sales, which tells you whether the company's products are gaining acceptance.

Then do the same thing with the operating income, which is income before taxes and unusual one-time expenses or profits, called "extraordinary items"; the per share net income; and the working capital. (Working capital is essentially the amount of money the company has on hand to finance its growth.) Repeat the process with the figures in the long-term comparison so you can come up with a trend line.

Also compare how much long-term debt, or liabilities, the company has versus its shareholders' equity and assets. Again, what you want to do is establish a pattern that tells you whether the company is paying off its debts or borrowing more than ever and whether its borrowing is within a normal range.

A few pages before or after this financial data chart, you'll find the "Statement of Cash Flow," which tells you how much money is coming in and how much is being spent. Another chart, which can be dubbed "Results of Operations" or "Consolidated Statement of Operations," notes where some of the money is being spent. For instance, is it going to research and development or general and administrative expenses? Is the company spending its money the same way it has in the past or has something changed?

After you've looked at all these numbers, you're likely to have questions. If everything has been rosy, you'll want to know if this trend can continue. If the company has started to borrow heavily, you'll want to know whether that's because it's in a major growth phase that could cause it to become more profitable than ever or because the company is disastrously short of cash. If some expense or revenue item has jumped out of its normal range, you'll want to know why simply so you can determine whether that's a positive or negative sign.

To find the answers to these questions, flip to the front of the report. There you'll see two things—a letter to shareholders, which is written by the chairman, chief executive, or president, followed by the "Management's Discussion and Analysis of Financial Condition and Operating Results," which in industry jargon is called the MD&A.

Here management explains what's happened to the company and the industry as a whole over the past year. It also discusses where the company thinks things are going and how it is responding to changes in its industry. Any balance sheet item that gave you pause should be mentioned here. If it's not, consider it a warning sign.

Last Step

THE FINAL THING you need to search for is something called the "footnotes" to the financial statement. In footnotes, the company explains its accounting, any significant estimates it has made, a description of the company's pension and employee benefit plans, and any other major assumption that was required to come up with the numbers you see in the annual report.

If there are significant legal actions pending, you should also expect to see a brief description of what they're about—and the types of risks they pose. Here you simply want to apply a reasonable-person standard to the information you see. If something seems off-kilter, you may want to investigate further, either by finding out how similar companies handle the same issue or by looking for analysts' reports.

Ferreting Out the Right Numbers in Financial Reports

H OW DO YOU DECIDE IF A STOCK IS WORTH BUYING? THERE ARE NO HARD AND FAST RULES, BUT THE FOL-lowing worksheet should help. The approach is based on the notion that the growth of a stock's price is a reflection of the company's growth in sales and earnings over time. However, to determine whether a stock is a buy from an investment stand-point, you need to ask a few questions. Then you need to do a lit-tle math to decide whether the price is reasonable.

WORKSHEET

Is It a Buy?

1 Does the cash produced by the company's operations cover its cost of doing business? You'll find the answer on the cash flow page of the company's annual report or 10K. If the cash produced from operations is insufficient to cover operating expenses, the company is likely to have to borrow or issue more stock. Either could prove detrimental to existing shareholders.

_____yes _____no

2 Has the company established a record of solid earnings growth? Can you see a pattern of rising earnings when looking at year-to-year comparisons in the company's 10K or financial statement?

_____yes _____no

95

3 Is there growing demand for the company's products?

_____yes _____no

4 Does the company produce a product or service that's difficult to duplicate? In other words, does it have technology or a particular expertise that will allow it to maintain a leading position in the industry for a long time?

_____yes _____no

5 Is the company's return on assets (ROA) 8 percent or more if it's a nonfinancial company or 1 percent or more for a bank, savings and loan, or insurer? (Companies normally publish an ROA in their financial statements. However, if it is not there, you can calculate it by dividing the company's total—not per share—earnings by total assets.) If the ROA is lower than these amounts, is it improving?

_____yes _____no

If you answered "yes" to all of those questions, you know you're looking at a good company. Now the question is whether its stock is selling at a reasonable price.

To figure that, do the calculations below:

Current market price	$_____
Annual earnings per share	$_____
Price-to-earnings (P/E) ratio	
(divide price by earnings per share)	= _____
Historical P/E*	= _____
Anticipated growth in earnings*	_____ %
Historical growth rate*	_____ %

*You can find these figures in the *Value Line Investment Survey*. This book, which has an annual subscription cost of $570, is available in most public libraries.

After completing the worksheet, compare today's P/E ratio to what it has been historically. If it's higher than normal, look at how today's earnings growth compares with the company's historic growth rate. If the growth rate is the same or lower than it has been in the past but the stock's P/E is higher, the stock's price is probably too expensive.

If the earnings growth rate is higher than normal, the stock can support a higher P/E multiple. The rule of thumb is that the stock's P/E can be as high as its expected growth rate. In other words, if a company is growing 30 percent per year, a 30 P/E wouldn't be too high. But do realize that as companies get bigger, double-digit growth rates become harder to sustain. A small company can sometimes double its sales and earnings for several years running. But once that company jumps from $10 million in sales to $100 million in sales, it's likely that its growth rate is going to taper off. When the company is at $1 billion in sales, it's likely to taper off dramatically. After all, increasing earnings by $10 million is a challenge, but increasing earnings by $1 billion in a single year is a miracle.

Finding Financial Data on the Web

T IMES HAVE CHANGED. WHEN DONNA TAKEDA STARTED WORKING ON WALL STREET IN THE EARLY 1970S, THE pinnacle of technology was the Dow Jones news wire, which tapped out one-line notes about per-share profits and losses when companies released their earnings. It took weeks before earnings were translated into analysts' reports, which were then mailed to investors.

If Takeda's clients wanted a market price for a stock, they had to call Takeda or hang out in a brokerage office, where they could watch the "ticker"—an electronic message board that reports trades a few minutes after they happen. When clients wanted to buy or sell stock, they called their brokers, too, and they expected each trade to cost from $100 to $500 in commissions. A few days or a week later, they would get a written statement that showed how much they had paid—or gotten—for their stock.

These days, Takeda can get earnings releases in real time and real detail the moment they're complete, and so can virtually any investor with a computer. Want a current market price? You can have it with a few keystrokes. To trade, all you need is a computer, an account, a modem, and, of course, some cash. Those costly trading commissions of yesteryear have shrunk to $8 to $30, depending on the discount broker. (You can certainly find brokers who charge more, but you're no longer forced to pay a fortune for each trade, so why would you?) And the trade is often completed and confirmed before you even sign off.

"The playing field is getting leveled, because the individual investor can see the information as quickly as we do," says Takeda, vice president of securities research and economics at Merrill Lynch & Co. in New York. "We all have access to the same information. The challenge is to figure out how to use all that information effectively."

Where do you go online to get company information and research? Dozens of sites offer everything from companies' annual reports to detailed technical analyses of individual stocks. Some sites allow you to register and then track your portfolio on a minute-by-minute basis. However, if you just need information—such as stock prices, ticker symbols, financial statements, and information about what managers are doing with their stock—there's no better place to go than Yahoo's finance site.

If you type http://finance.yahoo.com, you'll arrive at a site that asks you to feed in ticker symbols—the market abbreviations that are used when buying and selling stocks and mutual funds through an exchange. Don't know the ticker symbol? To the right of the window is a button called "symbol look-up." Click on it and then type the name of the company you want. If you have a full company name and you've spelled it correctly, you'll get the symbol. If you've typed a partial name and there are several possibilities, you'll get a list. Scroll down the list and click on the company you want.

Let's say you want to know about IBM. You click on "symbol look-up" and type IBM in the box. The response is a list of about a dozen symbols, many of which refer to IBM's preferred shares. You want the common shares, so you scroll down until you get to the simple "International Business Machines Corp." listing. The symbol turns out to be predictable. IBM. Click on it.

The next screen gives you a detailed look at IBM's daily trading activity, including the number of shares that changed hands that day; the normal trading volume; the fifty-two-week high and low; the company's earnings per share, P/E ratio, dividends, and dividend yield; and a chart that can be modified to show short- or long-term trend lines.

If you had done this on May 13, 1999, for example, you would have seen that IBM's stock had soared $20, closing at an all-time high of $246 on twice the normal trading volume—a hint that something was up. By clicking on "news" to bring up recent headlines and clicking again on any story you wanted to read in full, you would have read that IBM Chairman Louis Gerstner had said there was pent-up demand for the company's products because of rising acceptance of the Web. Gerstner isn't usually so positive, so the market reacted strongly.

But let's say you wanted to know more. What were the company's most recent earnings? Are company executives buying or selling IBM stock? What do securities analysts think of IBM? It's all there, with just a few more keystrokes.

Go back to the page with the IBM chart, and click on "research." This gives you analysts' ratings that rank the company on a scale of 1 to 5, with 1 recommending a "strong buy" and 5 meaning "strong sell." In a series of charts, this screen shows how many analysts are recommending the stock as a

1 = strong buy	**4** = moderate sell
2 = moderate buy	**5** = strong sell
3 = hold	

strong buy, a buy, a hold, and a sell. Analysts rarely say "sell," so anything neutral is considered relatively negative. In this case, IBM got high marks from the bulk of the analysts.

Hit the "back" icon at the top of your screen to return to the IBM chart, where there's another option called "profile." This takes you to a page that includes a brief company description, the names of top executives, a chart with pertinent earnings and cash flow data, and a lineup of links labeled "company news," "upgrade/-downgrade history," "latest stock price," "insider trades," "SEC filings," "investor relations," and "message board."

The message board is where a host of people—many of whom know less about IBM than you and/or your local video-store clerk do—tout or trash the company's stock. Consider this the electronic equivalent of cocktail-party chatter. If you feel curious, read it. But when you're considering an investment, ignore it unless you can tell who is posting the comments and you have reason to believe that they are reliable sources. In most instances, the people who post messages are anonymous. For all you know, they're company insiders, short-sellers (who profit when stock prices drop), or your local video-store clerk. Besides, you already know the company's news, as well as the stock price, the trend, and the analysts' views of IBM. You don't need the gossip.

The insider-trading history can give you a hint of how well company executives like the stock. However, because many executives receive discounted shares as part of their compensation packages, you should expect there to be more insider sales than purchases.

The insider-trading chart shows how the shares were bought—in other words, whether they were acquired via employee stock options or on the open market—and sold. Many analysts see open-market purchases as the most positive insider move. The insider trading screen can also be useful in tracking how many shares top officers continue to hold and whether, over time, they're adding to their holdings or divesting themselves of stock.

For in-depth earnings data, go back to the profile page and click on "SEC filings." There you can read everything from the company's latest annual and quarterly reports to its proxy statement, which details how officers are paid and what outside business relationships the company has with its directors.

The profile page also allows you to hook directly into IBM's own site, where you can learn about the company's history, its top officers, its financial results, and employment opportunities. Want to read a recent press release? Click on "news."

"It's all there," Takeda says. "Most analysts are using the Internet as a very useful source of information these days. And what we're looking at is virtually all the same information that you are seeing on Yahoo."

Technology Stocks

E ARLIER IN THIS CHAPTER, WE TALKED ABOUT HOW FUN-DAMENTALS DICTATE STOCK PRICES. NOW IT'S TIME to forget what you learned so we can talk about the recent notable exception: Internet stocks. Many of these companies had no earnings, management experience, or other fundamental indicators of value. What they had is potential—and stock prices that indicate that the sky was the limit.

Net Mania

"DOT-COM" STOCKS had risen so far so fast by late 1999 that many experts said we had entered a mania, a moment when market math temporarily goes out the window. When sanity returns, valuations plummet, laying waste to the millions of unsophisticated investors who bought Net stocks without questioning their true worth.

"The Internet is two different things," said Michael Murphy, editor of the *California Technology Stock Letter* and author of *Every Investor's Guide to High-Tech Stocks & Mutual Funds.* "In the real world, it is a fundamental paradigm shift in how we do business. In the financial world, it's a bubble."

Murphy's argument has proved all too true. However, investors who want to use the Internet mania as a model to avoid future investment mistakes must understand that there were plenty of respected experts singing the opposite tune.

Another contingent of market professionals believed that Net companies were so fundamentally different from businesses that rely on bricks and mortar—buildings, branch offices, and retail outlets—that their high stock valuations were reasonable. Even Internet naysayers said the rush to buy was not completely irrational. While past market manias saw investors snapping up tulips at irrational prices in seventeenth-century Holland, for example, underlying the Net fever was a belief that the Internet will change the world. Tulips have no long-term economic value, but the Net transcends time and space and makes it easier to reach customers, communicate, and transact business. Prices may have been steep, but some companies will eventually prosper and make their investors rich.

How expensive were Net stocks? Most stocks sell for ten to thirty times their current-year per-share earnings. In marketspeak, that's their price/earnings multiple. At the height of the mania, many Net stocks fetched *hundreds* of times—sometimes even *thousands* of times—their projected earnings.

"Is a 90 multiple—or a 300 multiple—for America Online too much? No," said Alexander C. Cheung, who managed the Monument Internet Fund at the time. Citing Amazon's zooming sales growth, Cheung said, "Amazon.com is only a five-year-old company. Can we use the same methodology to measure Amazon as Barnes & Noble or Wal-Mart? No."

Yet experts agreed that plenty of Internet stocks would not survive. Cheung, for example, figured that at least half of the Internet highfliers of 1998 and 1999 would be bankrupt in five to ten years. Which companies would fall and which would prosper was nearly impossible to say. The debate surrounding Amazon.com, the Internet-based seller of books, records, and tapes, crystallized the arguments on both sides. While the company's sales were soaring in 1999, so were its losses. The company had lost an astounding $1.2 billion since it was founded in 1994.

Still, investors poured in money. During 1999, Amazon.com's stock price soared from about $20 to an all time high of about $113. In early 2000, the price had settled in the $60 range, but that still gave this money loser a market capitalization—the value of all of the shares outstanding—of more than $20 billion. More recently, Amazon shares were trading in the single digits.

Why were investors so eager to buy this stock when other companies were more profitable? As Cheung put it, "You have to look at the business model, not just the business."

The Dot-com Business Model

AMAZON HAD ROUGHLY 10 million customers in early 2000. That was a big increase from a year earlier but still just a fraction of the roughly 125 million users of the World Wide Web. And, of course, the number of Web users is expected to continue growing at a blistering pace.

If Amazon's growth mirrored that of the Web, it would have 25 million customers by 2002 and sales of $2 billion, Cheung projected. But Amazon didn't plan to grow merely at the same pace as the Web. One reason the company lost so much money is that it aimed to be a "killer retailer"—such a recognized name that when people think books, they click on Amazon. The company was spending a small fortune on advertising, acquisitions, and customer service to gain a loyal following. Meanwhile, the company was expanding its offerings in an effort to leverage its name and infrastructure into more sales. If the strategy works, Amazon could become wildly profitable.

"When you cross that line, earnings could increase exponentially," Cheung said. "With a normal retailer, the profit margin is 2 percent to 4 percent of sales. But if you can do it without the brick and mortar, you can expect 5 percent to 6 percent."

Others questioned whether Amazon would ever see a profit. Virtually anyone with a computer, some programming expertise, and a connection with publishers can compete for book buyers, noted Alan F. Skrainka, chief market strategist with Edward Jones in St. Louis. Thus, the easiest way to gain market share when you're selling a commodity, such as books, CDs, or even stock trades, is to cut prices. That's good for consumers but rotten for profits, and ultimately it's bad for shareholders, he said.

"The Internet may soon be known as the great destroyer of profit margins," said Skrainka. "Companies that compete on price alone will not be able to earn a return for shareholders in the virtual marketplace."

Newsletter editor Murphy agreed. He expected other established booksellers that have already broken into the Web, including Barnes & Noble and some that promise to hit the Web soon, to erode Amazon's market share. Because the Web makes reaching consumers so simple, publishers might sell their books directly, he said. "A company like Amazon is probably never going to make any money," Murphy says. "I think they might as well change their name to Amazon.org." ("Org" is the Web designation for nonprofit groups.)

While the experts duke it out, it's up to investors to decide whom they believe—and whether they believe enough to put their savings in the shares of companies that have potential rather than established histories of profits.

Another Approach

IF YOU'RE NOT CONVINCED that Internet stocks are the way to go, or not convinced you can pick the potential winners from the losers, you might consider an alternate approach. Some experts believe you can profit from Net mania without actually jumping into dot-com stocks. How? You invest around the Web—or wait around a while.

For instance, you might want to think about shipping companies like Federal Express or UPS; printing companies such as Hewlett-Packard; phone firms such as MCI WorldCom; and data management and software companies such as Informix and Oracle.

Why? Very few prospectors got rich in the California gold rush, but the guys selling pans and jeans and meals to prospectors earned a fortune. In other words, you want to think about companies that benefit from the burgeoning of the Web without being officially Web-based companies. The reasons are twofold: First, some dot-com companies are selling for lofty prices, especially when you realize that only a handful of today's front-runners are likely to be top players in the future. Second, they're exposed to huge risks, because technology and competition among Web-based companies are changing so rapidly. It's likely that today's market leaders could be tomorrow's losers. But companies that facilitate Web-based commerce profit as long as there are companies going into and out of the Internet business.

Consider this: Before a Web-based company can launch, somebody has to buy a computer and a modem and hook into a telephone line. If they're selling anything, from books to clothes to plastic statuettes, they've got to ship those items to the consumer. That requires packaging and mailing—standard or express. And if the Web company manages to grow, it is probably going to need software to help it manage orders, customers, and inventory.

On the consumer's end, equipment is also needed to participate in the Web-based world—a computer, a modem, and a phone line.

And while you're at it, because so much of what's on the Web is worth printing—from greeting cards to photographs to fine art to recipes—why not a color printer too? At $100 or $200, a nice color printer is practically free, thrown into the package when you buy a computer. But those little ink cartridges cost $40 to $50 each. And if you print many greeting cards, you'll run through ink cartridges like water on a hot day.

Internet IPOs

BUT WHAT ABOUT Internet IPOs? Initial public offerings of Internet companies have gone wild since the late 1990s, often doubling and tripling in price on their very first day of trading. Isn't that where the action is?

This isn't traditional stock market investing. Traditionally, companies went public after they'd established a track record and, presumably, begun to post profits. The Internet companies that have come out in recent years often have little more to show for themselves than an idea and a prayer. Few have ever posted a profit. Some don't even have sales. Management experience? It's rare.

In a normal market, these companies would go to venture capitalists—rich investors who are willing to take a chance for a big piece of the eventual profits. However, in the late 1990s there was such demand for Internet stocks that individual investors were filling this role through the IPO process. Cheung suspects few individual investors realize that the risks are tremendous. "Venture capitalists do an incredible amount of homework. It's not, 'My cousin's sister's roommate told me that this was a great company,'" he says. Venture capitalists research industries to determine the potential; they take a careful look at the business plan and the management. They call the FBI and look up arrest records; they call the chief executive's high-school teachers to see what they have to say, Cheung quips. And even then, they expect to lose money on three out of every ten deals.

By contrast, individual investors were blindly jumping into Internet IPOs during the late 1990s boom years, often without a clue about what the company does, how it does it, and who is running it. That's a recipe for an exceptionally high eventual failure rate. "Individual investors have the mentality that they're not the financier, they're just trying to make a buck," he says. "But they are playing the role of the financier in a venture capital environment. They just don't have any idea what they are going to get."

Notably, past hot stock categories have followed a pattern, notes Skrainka. For instance, when the personal computer first came out in the 1970s, everybody wanted the "hot" computer companies—Apple, Commodore, and Eagle. When biotechnology became the rage in the early 1980s, people chased a host of now anonymous companies that were working on AIDS drugs, as well as a few companies, such as Amgen and Genentech, that have since proved their worth. If you'd waited to buy stock in these companies until both the market and the companies had settled down and established themselves, you wouldn't have made quite as much on the winners, but you wouldn't have lost on the losers, either.

"Nobody was asking about Intel and Dell in the early '80s," Skrainka says. "They were asking us about the market leaders, which were Commodore and Osborne."

Everyone wants to get in on the ground floor. However, Intel went public in 1971; Microsoft went public in 1986; Compaq in 1982. If you had waited to buy shares in each until 1990, you still would have earned average annual returns that ranged from 400 percent to 37 percent—not half bad.

"Instead of rushing in, bide your time. Wait for the leaders to emerge," Skrainka advises. "Yes, you will leave some money on the table. But you will vastly increase your chances of success."

chapter 6

Tough Sell

M|ANY OF THE NATION'S top investors have one common credo: Buy good companies and hold them long-term. Billionaire investor Warren Buffett goes a step further. He suggests you buy good companies and hold them "forever."

But everyone makes an occasional mistake. Knowing when to cut and run can be as important as knowing what to buy. Still, even professional investors acknowledge that determining when to sell is tough, for reasons both psychological (it's hard to admit you've erred) and practical (you must keep a close eye on your portfolio).

"Knowing when to sell is probably the most difficult thing to do," says Ralph Bloch, technical analyst with Raymond James Financial Inc. in St. Petersburg, Florida. "Most people stay with the existing trend too long."

However, determining when—or whether—you should sell is easier if you spend some time each quarter keeping up with your investments and occasionally subjecting them to the detailed analysis that you conducted when determining which stocks to buy.

Keeping an Eye
on the Financials

T O DO THIS WITH A MINIMUM OF TIME AND EFFORT, MAKE A POINT OF LOOKING AT THE QUARTERLY STATEMENTS you receive. Publicly held companies send out statements every three months that show how their sales and earnings have fared over the period compared with the preceding three months and the year-ago quarter. The statement also includes a message from the chief executive or chairman that briefly describes the factors that contributed to the quarter's results.

Wise investors take a look at just a few key elements, such as, profit, strategies, and extraordinary items. On the profit side, investors want to look at year-to-year comparisons of net earnings. Year-to-year earnings comparisons are usually better than quarter-to-quarter comparisons, because many companies are subject to cyclical swings. A retailer, for example, is likely to post a higher profit in the final quarter of the year—Christmas season—than the following quarter. Consequently, to accurately gauge this company's growth, you must compare fourth quarter with fourth quarter, first quarter with first.

When making the comparisons, ask: Are net earnings growing as fast as you expected when you purchased the stock? If they're not—no matter whether the earnings are much higher or much lower—you need to ask why.

For instance, has a one-time event, such as the sale of a profitable subsidiary, boosted near-term profits to the detriment of long-term results? Or has the company simply found more efficient ways to operate, which are likely to make it even richer over the long term? The answer to that question determines whether you should consider selling now or whether you should consider buying more shares.

If earnings have been disappointing, the analysis is the same. Are earnings down because the company is retooling to accommodate strong growth? Or is it because demand is slack or competition is stiff?

The answers to those questions are likely to be found in the chairman's message right at the beginning of the report. If the numbers you've reviewed—and that message—leave you with continued positive feelings about the company's prospects, hang tight. Consider yourself a budding Buffett and keep a firm grip on your shares.

What About Stock Price Movement?

BUT SHOULDN'T YOU CHECK THE STOCK PRICE BEFORE YOU DECIDE TO HOLD? EVEN IF THE COMPANY'S FUNDA-mentals are sound, doesn't it make sense to sell when the stock price has risen a set amount?

Probably not. If you sell to lock in a profit and the stock is not held in an individual retirement account or other tax-favored retirement plan, you've also locked in a taxable gain. In addition, you'll pay trading costs to sell and purchase new shares. Ultimately, your next investment must be substantially better than the first, once you account for the tax and trading costs. Consequently, many seasoned investors advise that you ignore the day-to-day price movements as long as you are convinced of the stock's fundamental value.

Of course, there are always exceptions, such as those "hot" stocks selling in "hot" industries. On occasion, the value of a high-flying stock will get so out of whack that reasonable investors would have to conclude that it makes some sense to take their profits and invest their money elsewhere. Still, for those who were lucky enough to enjoy that type of appreciation in a very short time, it still may make sense to hold on for a few extra months. Why? You need to hold a stock for more than a year to qualify for long-term capital gains tax rates on the profit. Those capital gains rates can sometimes save you so much versus paying tax at your ordinary income tax rate that you can suffer a fairly substantial loss on the stock and still come out better off for waiting.

Otherwise, look at the stock price only when the company's earnings are troubling and the chairman's message gives you further pause. At that point, you use the current market price to calculate the firm's price-to-earnings ratio. You then evaluate its future prospects for growth by consulting the *Value Line Investment Survey.*

As described in Chapter 5, the price/earnings (P/E) ratio can be calculated by simply dividing the current market price by the annualized earnings per share. If the resulting figure is less than the five-year projected earnings growth rate in Value Line, it may be best to hang on.

If, however, the P/E is higher than the projected growth rate, it's a signal that the stock price could decline. Naturally, you can hang on and hope for a recovery. But before you do, ask "Is my money better invested elsewhere?" and the corollary question,

"Would I buy this stock today?"

It makes sense to hold on to a lackluster performer only if you think your prospects with other investments aren't any better. Holding on because you've suffered a loss and want to "get even" before selling only serves to put you farther behind, investment professionals say.

Consider Mary, who bought 100 shares of XYZ Co. at $10 each but then saw the per-share price drop to $7, leaving her with a $300 loss. She decides to hang on, waiting for a recovery. Five years later, the share price does climb back to $10. But Mary shouldn't consider that breaking even.

If she had sold five years earlier and reinvested $650 (the stock's $700 value, minus a $50 trading fee—there is no tax when you have no profit) in another company that appreciated 10 percent annually, she would have had $1,069.45. Had Mary's initial investment been $100,000 instead of $1,000, that $69 she'd forgone would amount to $6,945. In other words, the more you have invested, the more it hurts to stick with a loser.

Tax Implications
of Selling at a Profit

YOU UNDERSTAND THAT YOU OUGHT TO SELL YOUR LOSERS, BUT WHAT ABOUT THOSE WINNERS? EVERY once in a while, an investor strikes it big in a big hurry.

Consider those who invested in Qualcomm stock at the beginning of 1999, when the company was selling for $28 per share. By late November, the stock price had soared to a stunning $372. Meanwhile, analysts who had touted Qualcomm's stock when it was selling for 40 times earnings were considerably less enthusiastic about the company's appreciation potential when the stock started selling for 290 times current-year profits.

Yet if an investor was holding the shares in a taxable account at the end of 1999 and had owned the stock for less than a year, he'd be wise to do a little math before selling. Why? If you sell stocks that you've owned for less than a full twelve months, you pay federal tax at your ordinary income tax rate rather than the lower capital gains rate. Even for somebody in a fairly modest tax bracket, that difference can amount to thousands of dollars. But what if the stock's price drops before your one-year anniversary? You may still be better off if you wait. Indeed, a middle-income investor could suffer about a 10 percent loss on his or her shares and still end up better off, after tax, by waiting for the lower capital gains rate.

To illustrate, consider two hypothetical investors: John Average, who is in the 28 percent federal tax bracket, and Gina Gotrocks, who pays 36 percent of her income in federal tax. They each bought 100 shares of Qualcomm stock in January 1999, when it was selling for $28 a share. But by Thanksgiving, Qualcomm was selling for a stunning $372, leaving these investors with taxable gains of $344 per share.

If John sold at Thanksgiving, he'd pay tax at his ordinary income tax rate, which would cost him $9,632 in federal tax. If he waited until January, and Qualcomm's stock managed to maintain its value, he would pay just $6,880 in tax, or $2,752 less.

But what if the stock price fell in the interim? John could actually suffer a $34 per share decline in the value of his Qualcomm stock and still end up ahead, after tax, thanks to the lower capital gains rates. No kidding. If he sold at Thanksgiving, he would cash out with $37,200. But after paying the $9,632 in federal income tax, he pockets just $27,568. On the other hand, if he waited and the stock dropped to $338 in the interim, he would pay $6,200 in federal tax and walk away with $27,600—$32 more—after tax.

What about Gina? She'd have to lose more than $68 per share on the stock—in other words, Qualcomm's stock price would have to drop from Thanksgiving's $372 to $304—before she'd be better off selling then rather than waiting for the lower capital gains rate. If she sold at Thanksgiving, she'd pay $12,384 in federal tax—that's 36 percent of her $34,400 gain—and go home with $24,816 after tax. If she sold at $304 the following February, she'd pay just $5,520 in federal capital gains taxes and go home with $24,880.

Incidentally, Qualcomm's case also graphically illustrates another reason to hang on. In late December the company's stock split four-for-one. By March 2000 the company's shares were selling for the equivalent of $525 on a presplit basis. John and Gina were well rewarded for a few months of waiting.

Figuring the Break-Even Sales Price

HOW DO YOU FIGURE THE BREAK-EVEN POINT? TO DO IT RIGHT REQUIRES HIGH-SCHOOL ALGEBRA THAT MOST investors have long since forgotten. However, for the nostalgic, here is how to calculate the break-even sales price: Take the net after-tax sales proceeds (assuming you're paying tax at ordinary income tax rates) and subtract the product of the long-term capital gains rate and your tax basis in the stock, then divide that number by one minus the long-term capital gains rate.

You followed that, right?

Never fear, you can come up with a fairly accurate guesstimate by simply comparing the tax you'd pay on each share at ordinary income tax rates to the tax at long-term capital gains rates—assuming that the stock price stays steady. With Gina, for example, you know that she'd pay roughly $124 in federal tax on every share that she sold at $372 in November. (The sales price of $372 minus the $28 she paid equals $344, times 36 percent equals $123.86, which I rounded off to $124.) If she waits until February to get the lower 20 percent rate, she pays just $68.80 per share in tax. The $55 difference tells you she can easily suffer a $55 per share loss on Qualcomm's price without suffering any after-tax loss to her pocketbook.

Of course, this method understates the real impact. (In reality, if you wait and get less for your shares, you have a lower profit, and that means you pay even less in tax.) But it's a far cry simpler for those who prefer a back-of-the-envelope calculation to algebra.

For those who prefer the accuracy of algebra, here's the formula:

$$\frac{ATP - (LTCG)(TB)}{1 - (LTCG)} = BESP$$

BESP = Break-even sales price

ATP = After-tax proceeds from the sale at your ordinary income tax rate

LTCG = Long-term capital gains rate of 20 percent (0.20)

TB = Your tax basis in the stock

Let's fill in some numbers from Gina's example to see if it gets clearer. Gina paid $28 per share for her stock. If she sold at $372, her taxable gain would be $344 (the difference between the cost and the sales price). Multiply that amount by her ordinary income tax rate of 36 percent. She'd pay $123.84 in federal tax on each share she sold. That would leave her with net after-tax sales proceeds of $248.16. You plug that number in where it says ATP (after-tax proceeds). Now multiply the long-term capital gains rate of 20 percent (0.20) by her tax basis in the stock of $28. The result: $5.60. Subtract $5.60 from $248.16 to get $242.56.

Finally, divide $242.56 by the inverse of the long-term capital gains rate, which is 80 percent, or 0.80. The result: $303.20, which I rounded up to $304. That's the break-even point. As long as she sells her stock for more than $303.20, she's ahead by waiting for the lower capital gains rate.

Here's how Gina's formula looks:

$$248.16 - (0.20 \times \$28 = \$5.60) = 242.56 \div 0.80 = \$303.20$$

The worksheet below provides the formula for you to use with numbers from your portfolio.

WORKSHEET

Figuring the Tax Implications of Selling Too Soon

1 To determine how much you would net (after tax) if you sold stock today, first compute the sales price minus the original cost of the investment, to get your net proceeds.

_____ — _____ = _____
(sales price)   (original cost of Investment)   (net proceeds)

2 Now multiply the net proceeds by your ordinary income tax rate (0.28, 0.31, 0.36, or 0.396) to get the after tax proceeds.

_____ x _____ = _____
(net proceeds)   (ordinary income tax rate)   (after tax proceeds)

3 Put the resulting after tax proceeds in the space marked #1 below.

[#1] $_____ — (0.20 x [#2] $_____) —
      (after tax proceeds)   (0.20 x (original cost of investment))

[#3] $_____
       (result)

(continued)

4 Plug in the amount that you originally paid for the stock in space #2 on the preceding page.

5 Multiply the long-term capital gains rate (0.20) by the number in space #2, and subtract the result from the number you plugged into space #1.

6 Plug the result into space #3 on the preceding page.

7 Now divide #3 by 0.80 in the space below. The result is your break-even sales price.

[#3] $_____ / 0.80 = $_____

(result from above formula) / 0.80 = (break-even sales price)

chapter 7

Investing
in Bonds

T HE STOCK MARKET'S dazzling performance over much of the past decade convinced most investors that equities are worth owning. But the same can't be said of bonds. Their yields had been lackluster in recent years. Moreover, those who bought long-term bonds for what they thought would be fairly stable total returns have been sorely disappointed. Long-term bonds have posted as many years of negative total returns in the past three decades as small-company stocks, which have long been considered the most speculative and volatile of traditional domestic investments.

Yet bonds—or at least some type of fixed-income investment, ranging from long-term corporate bonds to shorter-term government notes, bills, money markets, and certificates of deposit—are a must for most investor portfolios. Why? Fixed-income instruments address certain financial goals better than any other investment. And despite the prevalent urge to act as if investing is a high-stakes contest in which the winners are the people who post the highest gains, remember your mantra. Having the amount of money you need when you need it is the name of this game.

The fact is, while U.S. stocks have posted higher average annual returns than any other type of financial asset over long periods of time, they're a miserable place to put short- and medium-term money. That's because stock prices gyrate wildly in short periods of time. And sometimes stock prices can stay down for periods ranging from five to fifteen years. If the money you're investing is aimed at satisfying an important goal in the meantime, you're out of luck.

Fixed-income instruments are ideal to address those short- and medium-term goals for a simple reason, says Kenneth J. Taubes, codirector of the fixed-income group at Pioneer Investment Management in Boston. Ninety percent of the return on a fixed-income instrument comes from the "coupon," or the interest paid on your initial investment, not from price appreciation. That makes them perfect for people who need to generate cash from their investments to supplement their monthly income. And it makes them a perfect investment for someone with an important goal that must be satisfied with a set amount of cash within five years or so.

Fixed Income Choices

T HE TYPE OF FIXED-INCOME INVESTMENT THAT BEST SERVES YOUR NEEDS DEPENDS ON YOUR INCOME AND circumstances. For instance, if you need current income, you may want to take a look at corporate bonds or, if you're in a high tax bracket, tax-free municipals. Both offer better after-tax returns than U.S. Treasury bonds, the bellwether bond noted for the promise of complete security of your principal if you hold the bond to maturity.

At a time when thirty-year Treasury bonds would yield about 6 percent, you would expect to get 8 percent or more on higher- and medium-risk corporate bonds. Those better returns mean you can live more comfortably. It is the difference between getting $6,000 annually on your $100,000 investment and getting $8,000 or even $10,000. But you have to recognize that corporate bonds also pose more risk to your principal. After all, it's more likely that a company will have difficulty paying its bills and bondholders than the U.S. government, which can raise taxes or easily borrow more if it falls short of cash.

As a result, experts suggest that if you invest in corporate bonds, do it through a mutual fund, which gives you wide diversification and the benefit of professional management and clout. (When bond-issuing companies get into hot water, they often invite their biggest investors to the table to help work out a repayment plan. Individuals rarely get such invitations, and they usually lack the skill and clout to make the most of such meetings if they did.)

Municipal bonds, which are issued by state and local governments and agencies, offer less generous interest rates than corporate bonds, but you usually get to keep all the money. Most types of municipal bonds are exempt from federal income tax and—for in-state residents—state taxes as well. For someone in the highest tax brackets, it doesn't take much return to make this a great deal.

Consider that for those in a combined marginal tax bracket of 45 percent—this applies to Californians earning $250,000 or more per year—getting a 5 percent tax-free return is the equivalent of getting a 9.09 percent return on a taxable bond. For example, if an investor in the 45 percent tax bracket plopped $10,000 into a bond earning 9.09 percent, he'd come away with $909 at year-end. However, he'd then have to pay 45 percent of that—$409—to federal and state taxing authorities. That leaves him with just $500, or a 5 percent after-tax yield on his investment. That 9.09 percent is called the "taxable equivalent yield," and it is the basis by which municipal bonds are usually sold.

To figure a taxable equivalent yield, divide the interest rate by the inverse of your combined state and federal tax rate. (You can estimate your tax rate if you don't know it, since a percentage point or two won't matter much.) In the above example, that means you divide 5 by 0.55—1 minus the 45 percent (0.45) combined tax rate—to get 9.09.

On the other hand, if you've got a child going to college in a year or two and you need most of the first year's tuition money ready and available without risk to your principal, you'd be better served with a money market account. Money markets offer relatively paltry yields, but they invest in short-term government and corporate securities that are both safe and easily accessible. That makes such accounts, which can be opened with mutual funds or banks, ideal places to park short-term money that you can't afford to lose.

Or you could choose a Treasury note, which is like a bond, but it matures—or pays back the principal—in two to five years. Pick a note that matures when your goal needs to be satisfied.

If you are an investor who can handle a higher default risk, boost your returns by buying comparatively riskier securities, such as a junk-bond fund (also known as high-yield funds). If you're looking for lower risk, on the other hand, stick with

Treasuries with short maturities—those that will pay back the principal in five years or less.

In many cases, investors would be wise to diversify their bond portfolios just as they diversify their stock holdings. For example, if you have a substantial bond portfolio, put a portion in junk or international bonds, a portion in Treasuries, and perhaps a portion in municipal bonds or mortgage-backed securities. The Treasury portion will keep a bit of your principal safe, whereas the junk portion will boost the return. The municipals can give you decent tax-free income, whereas the mortgage-backed securities offer guaranteed repayment of principal and somewhat higher interest rates than other guaranteed investments.

Bonds for Diversification

L ET'S SAY YOU HAVE NO SPECIFIC SHORT-TERM GOAL, BUT YOU WONDER WHETHER YOU OUGHT TO HAVE A BIT— perhaps just 10 percent—of your portfolio in bonds, solely for diversification's sake? Absolutely, experts maintain.

The last time the U.S. stock market went through a sustained down period, in the 1970s, the return on two-year Treasury notes—one of the dullest fixed-income investments—handily outpaced that of stocks for a full decade. In 1982, when interest rates were finally beginning to drop after hitting historic highs, the Standard and Poor's 500 stock index posted a healthy 21.6 percent return. But the return on thirty-year Treasury bonds was far better—43.6 percent—thanks to falling interest rates that sharply boosted the price of those bonds, says Joan Payden, chief executive of Payden & Rygel, a Los Angeles–based money management firm. "We are always tainted by what happened last," Payden says. "But at some point in time, bonds will do better than stocks."

It's important to realize that bonds and stocks can sometimes move in the same direction at the same time, but rarely do they move at the same pace. Sometimes returns on stocks and bonds move in opposite directions, which makes them an ideal duo for smoothing the bumps in your investment portfolio—the main point of diversification.

Risks

H OW DO THE RISKS AND REWARDS OF BONDS COMPARE WITH THOSE OF STOCKS? WHEN YOU INVEST IN BONDS, you are effectively lending the issuer money. In return, the issuer promises to pay back your principal at some time in the future and to pay a set rate of interest for as long as the bond is outstanding. Consequently, you face two risks—default and interest rate fluctuations.

Default risk is the chance that the issuer—be it a government or a corporation—will get into financial hot water and be unable to pay all or part of the principal or interest. The amount of default risk varies dramatically with the type of security you buy. Treasury notes and bonds are believed to be virtually free of default risk, because the U.S. government is highly creditworthy. The default risk on debt issued by highly indebted companies or Third World countries, on the other hand, is fairly substantial.

Because risk and reward go hand in hand, an investor who can handle uncertainty can usually boost the yield on a bond portfolio by investing a portion of it in securities that pose some default risk. Generally speaking, junk bonds—that is, below-investment-grade securities, often issued by heavily indebted corporations—and bonds issued by Third World countries pay between 3 and 10 percentage points more than debt issued by the U.S. Treasury. (If you buy foreign bonds, you must also beware of "currency risk," which is explained in more detail in Chapter 10.)

Interest rate risk crops up when inflation and interest rates are rising. A long-term bond bought in the early 1980s, when interest rates were high, yields much more than a bond bought today, and one bought in a time of lower interest rates yields much less. Thus, the price on that higher-yielding bond will rise, and the price on the lower-yielding bond will drop.

How much it will drop depends on the bond's maturity—the amount of time the issuer has before it must pay back the principal—and the difference between current interest rates and the return on the bond. According to an analysis by Oppenheimer, a New York–based mutual fund company, the estimated value of a two-year Treasury note will decrease by about 2 percent if interest rates rise 1 percentage point, but the value of a bond that matures in twenty years will decline by about 8 percent.

If you invest in bond mutual funds, which post their net asset values each day, you will see the effect of rising interest rates on your funds immediately. However, if you invest in individual bonds, you may not notice. That's simply because no one "marks their bonds to market"—that is, no one tells you the price you'd get if you were selling the bond today. Unless, of course, you ask. So if you want to stay relatively oblivious to the value bumps in your bond holdings, invest in individual bonds. If you want liquidity and don't mind knowing when the bond market declines, buy bonds through mutual funds.

chapter 8

Mutual Funds

DON'T HAVE THE TIME, skill, or interest to pick individual stocks? There's no need to give up on investing. You can get a professional to do the stock picking for you. The easiest and least-expensive way to do that is to build a portfolio of mutual funds. If you choose funds wisely, not only can you save time, you also can enjoy steady returns.

But first, a little deprogramming may be necessary for those who frequent magazine stands. There are no "Best Funds to Buy Now." There is no one-size-fits-all "Fund

Portfolio for the New Millennium." Indeed, the hottest funds of today are frequently the coldest funds of tomorrow. Buy them at your economic peril. "There is more risk of loss when you buy a fund that's at the top of the performance charts than there is when you buy a fund at the bottom," says A. Michael Lipper, chairman of Lipper Inc., a mutual fund information and ranking service based in New York.

So how do you pick good funds? First, a little background is required.

What is a Mutual Fund?

M UTUAL FUNDS ARE INVESTMENT POOLS THAT COLLECT MONEY FROM MANY INVESTORS AND USE IT TO BUY stocks, bonds, and other investments. The type of securities the fund buys is spelled out in a detailed investment document called a prospectus. Each investor then owns a pro-rata share of the assets in the pool.

The fund company employs an investment manager, who chooses the specific stocks or bonds to buy and sell based on criteria spelled out in the prospectus. Open-ended mutual funds—which make up the bulk of the industry—also calculate the value of the pool's investment holdings each day, divide that by the number of shares owned by individual investors, and report the result—the net asset value of each share. Most of these net asset values are reported in major newspapers each day, just like the prices of individual stocks. You can also get mutual fund quotes on financial Web sites, such as Yahoo! Finance (see "Finding Financial Data on the Web," in Chapter 5). And many major fund families also provide these quotes on their Web sites.

On the other hand, "closed-end" funds sell a specific number of shares to investors at launch and don't sell additional shares.

The shares of closed-end funds then trade on stock exchanges, much like the shares of individual stocks. Sometimes their shares sell for more than the market value of all the securities owned by the fund; sometimes they sell for less. Because of this, you would pick closed-end funds in much the same way as you'd choose an individual stock rather than a mutual fund. As a result, all of the rest of this chapter refers to open-end mutual funds only.

Over the past decade or so, the ranks of mutual fund owners have burgeoned. Where roughly 20 million Americans invested through mutual funds in 1986, some 77 million invested this way at the turn of the millennium. Assets held by fund companies soared to some $6 trillion by 2000 from $810.3 billion in 1986.

What's made mutual funds so popular? They make investing easy. You buy a fund with a general mission and let the manager worry about exactly what stocks or bonds to buy and when to sell. After all, that's the fund manager's business—and you can feel comfortable going about your own.

The other compelling draw of mutual funds is the fact that they allow you to diversify even a small investment portfolio in a cost-effective way. When you buy a share in a mutual fund, you are buying a piece of all of the securities the fund owns. For example, a growth fund typically owns dozens—sometimes hundreds—of different stocks in different industries. An income, or bond, fund is likely to own a wide array of bonds and/or other fixed-income instruments with different maturities. Most funds also keep some assets in cash, both to pay off customers who decide to sell their fund shares and to buy better investment opportunities as they arise. For you to get the same amount of diversification that a fund buyer could get with a $5,000 investment, you would need a portfolio worth at least several hundred thousand dollars.

Fees and Loads

W HAT DOES IT COST TO GET THIS DIVERSIFICATION? THAT DEPENDS ON WHETHER YOU ARE BUYING A SO-CALLED load or a no-load fund.

In a nutshell, a load is a fee that's either charged when you buy the shares (a "front-end load") or when you sell them in the first few years (a "back-end load"). These fees go to pay the financial planners and stockbrokers who sell the fund. In the best cases, the planners and stockbrokers earn the fees by giving you good advice about which fund or funds to choose, based on your age, goals, and the other details of your portfolio. Unfortunately, in the worst cases, the planners don't give good advice—they just recommend funds that pay them rich commissions. Your portfolio suffers while the planner buys a Jaguar. (But I'm hopeful that you'll learn enough by reading this book to avoid that.)

There is one other reason that a fund might charge a load: volatility. Certain types of funds, most commonly international and market-segment funds (see the description of sector funds in "Picking Funds for Your Portfolio," later in this chapter), charge loads mainly to discourage investors from short-swing trading. That's because these fund managers know that the value of the fund's portfolio is likely to swing wildly simply because of the nature of the securities the fund buys. To keep investors locked in through the bad times, so they can enjoy the good and so the managers won't have to sell assets to raise cash to pay off selling fund holders at the worst time, they charge back-end loads that are only levied on those who sell out within a certain period—usually within the first three to five years.

No-load funds do not charge "loads," but some charge 12b-1 fees. These also go to pay the planner or broker who recommends the fund, but they are a bit more insidious. Instead of costing you a fairly obvious amount when you buy or sell your shares, 12b-1 fees are charged annually, usually in relatively small amounts. However, for long-term investors, they can cost more than even a substantial load.

And every type of mutual fund charges something called "annual management fees," which are the costs that you pay for the service of having a professional do the investment picking for you. The cost of trading—buying and selling stocks in the fund portfolio—also gets passed through to you through "other" fees.

By and large, all fund fees are charged as a percentage of your investment. If you buy a fund with a 5 percent front-end load, for example, 5 percent of the amount you invest is taken off the top. Instead of investing $100 in the fund, you actually invest $95. With a back-end load, the fee is charged when you sell. So if you sell $1,000 worth of shares in a fund with a 3 percent back-end load, the fund company will take $30 and send you $970.

With 12b-1 and annual management fees, the costs are taken out of your annual return before it's passed on to you. So let's say you pay 1 percent in annual management fees, and your fund earns 10 percent. You get a 9 percent return on your money. What happens if your fund just barely breaks even? You lose 1 percent on your money. (For an explanation of exactly how much these fees can cost you and a nifty tool to help you examine the total cost of the fees that your funds are charging, see the last section of this chapter.)

The good news is that all the fees that a fund charges must be disclosed in a chart in the fund prospectus. No-load funds automatically send you a copy of the prospectus when you say you want to invest. However, if you are buying a load fund from a broker, you may need to ask for it. Make sure you do.

The Prospectus

P ROSPECTUSES ARE LONG, BORING LEGAL DOCUMENTS THAT SPELL OUT ALL THE DETAILS ABOUT INVESTING IN a particular fund. Like most long, boring legal documents, they contain a handful of fascinating tidbits of information that can tell you whether the investment you're looking at is likely to be a boon or a bust before you put your money at risk.

Besides the fees, what else should you be looking for in the prospectus?

Performance

EVERY PROSPECTUS MUST SUMMARIZE how the fund has performed over a variety of time periods. Somewhere in the legalese, it also tells you that "past performance is not an indication (or guarantee) of future returns." That's true. A fund that makes a fortune in one year can lose a fortune the next. What you need to know about performance is the predictable part. That's volatility.

Look at the figures that show average annual returns over one-year, five-year, and ten-year time periods. Compare those returns to the returns of an appropriate market index. For instance, the performance of a fund that invests in big-company stocks can be compared to the Standard and Poor's 500 stock market index. That tells you whether your fund manager generally does better, worse, or about the same as the markets he's investing in as a whole.

Also look for the year-by-year performance. If you can't find it, ask for a chart showing this data before you invest. Why is it so important? It tells you whether the fund you are looking at has relatively stable returns or whether the averages you've seen are masking a lot of volatility. For instance, a fund that clicks along earning 7 to 9 percent per year is significantly different from a fund that posts an "average" 8 percent return but has some years where it earns 40 percent and others where it loses half its value. This knowledge can help you determine just how likely you are to suffer a loss (or an ulcer) before you cash out.

Certainly, if you are capable of handling risk, don't eliminate highly volatile funds from consideration. But make sure you look at these figures before you invest so that you are prepared. The biggest mistake that a fund investor can make is investing in a volatile fund without understanding the swings. Then, chances are, when the fund posts a terrible year—as volatile funds are sure to do sooner or later—the unprepared investor sells out. Often that means selling at the absolute worst point, locking in a loss with a fund that's simply a roller coaster, ready to rise back after dumping the unprepared at the bottom.

Investment Objectives

EACH PROSPECTUS also discloses what the fund is investing in and why. Primarily all you are looking for here is to make sure you've chosen the right type of fund for your investment objectives. For instance, if you want to put your long-term retirement money in small-company stocks, you'd look for a fund that invests its assets in the shares of small public companies. Similarly, if you want a short-to-medium-term bond fund for your teen's college account, you'd check the prospectus to determine whether the manager has such bonds in the fund's portfolio.

Risks

BY AND LARGE, the paragraphs labeled "risk" in the average fund prospectus are boilerplate. In essence, they say that investments involve risk. Stocks go up; stocks go down. So do bond prices. Live with it.

Every once in a while, however, the risk disclosures tell you more. If, for example, the fund uses leverage to boost its returns, it is noted here. What that means is the fund manager is borrowing so he can buy more stock than he can afford with the cash he has on hand. Unless you're prepared for much bigger price swings than the normal fund of this type, avoid funds that leverage their positions.

International funds tell you about their "hedging" strategies that are aimed at reducing currency risk (see Chapter 10). Some funds will say they don't hedge currency risk. Others say that they do and explain how. Typically, the funds that hedge earn a little less than the funds that don't when currency prices are in your favor, but they should earn more than those that don't when currency prices go the other way.

Picking Funds for Your Portfolio

I F FUNDS WILL MAKE UP THE BULK OF YOUR INVESTMENT PORTFOLIO, YOU SHOULD DIVERSIFY AMONG DIFFERENT types of investment classes—big-company stocks, small-company stocks, international investments, bonds, and cash. That means you probably need at least five different funds.

In fundspeak, big-company stocks are sometimes categorized as "growth" or "growth and income" funds; small-company stocks are sometimes labeled "aggressive growth"; bond funds are usually listed under "income." Fortunately, there's no special code for money market and international funds. You'll find them predictably labeled. However, you should know that "global" or "world" funds differ from "international" or "foreign" funds in that the former two categories can invest domestically as well as in foreign markets. The latter are restricted to overseas investments.

You should diversify among all these categories for two reasons. The first is that a good investment portfolio addresses the purpose of your savings—the specific goals you aim to finance. Some of your goals may be short-term, some long-term, some pivotal, some discretionary. To appropriately address an important short-term goal, you need a short-term investment, such as a money market fund, that is not going to put your principal in great jeopardy. To address your long-term goals, you're better served with stock funds (either "growth" or "aggressive growth"), which swing in value but are more likely to handily outpace inflation over time.

Your fund-type choices boil down to the following options:

❏ **Aggressive growth funds** usually consist of stocks in small, fast-growing companies. Most of these companies do not pay dividends, and their stock prices are highly volatile.

Risk: Very high
Potential for capital appreciation: Very high
Potential for current income: Low

❏ **Asset-allocation funds** are often called "funds of funds" because they purchase shares in an array of different types of mutual funds—stock, bond, money market, and international, for example—in order to completely diversify an investor's holdings. The concept behind asset-allocation funds is that one fund can be enough for your entire portfolio.

Risk: Mixed
Potential for capital appreciation: Moderate
Potential for current income: Mixed

❏ **Balanced funds** aim for three things: income, growth of capital, and stability of principal. They do this by buying a mixture of stocks, bonds, and money market instruments.

Risk: Moderate
Potential for capital appreciation: Moderate
Potential for current income: Mixed

❑   **Fixed-income funds** invest in bonds and other fixed-income instruments, such as mortgage-backed securities. There are a wide array of different types of fixed-income funds, ranging from funds that invest in high-grade debt, such as Treasury notes and bonds, to those that invest in the debt of highly indebted companies (junk-bond funds). Obviously, the risk to your principal hinges on what type of securities your fund buys. However, all fixed-income funds face interest-rate risk, as described in Chapter 7. In a nutshell, if interest rates rise, the value of your old, relatively low-yielding bonds will fall. If interest rates drop, the value of your old, relatively high-yielding bonds will rise. But when you buy individual bonds, you're relatively blind to the changes in market direction—no one calls you to tell you that your bond is worth less or more than what you paid on a day-to-day basis. As discussed earlier, though, mutual funds report their net asset values every single day. So if you've got a paper loss on your bond fund, you'll know it. These paper losses should not negatively affect the income you receive, so if you are investing mainly for income, you shouldn't let them bother you. But expect to see them, because interest rates do change and will affect the fund's net asset values.
Risk: Moderate
Potential for capital appreciation: Low to moderate
Potential for current income: High

❑   **Equity-income funds** invest primarily in stocks that pay high dividends. These present some potential for capital appreciation but much less stability than a balanced fund or than many types of fixed-income funds.
Risk: Moderate
Potential for capital appreciation: Low to moderate
Potential for current income: Moderate

❑   **Global funds** invest in securities issued all over the world—foreign and domestic. International funds invest in non-U.S. markets. Because the cost of trading in overseas markets is comparatively high, you should expect these funds to charge slightly higher fees than domestic stock funds. Also, international markets, particularly those in developing nations, tend to be more volatile than the U.S. market, so you should expect bigger changes in your net asset values.

Risk: High

Potential for capital appreciation: High

Potential for current income: Low (except with bond funds)

❑   **Growth funds** consist of stocks in larger, more established U.S. companies. Stock prices are volatile; however, the price of shares in established companies is comparatively less volatile than the price of shares in small, untested companies. Consequently, growth funds are a bit less risky than aggressive growth funds.

Risk: High

Potential for capital appreciation: Moderate

Potential for current income: Low

❑   **Growth and income funds** combine growth stocks with stocks in companies that pay high dividends. Some growth and income funds also invest in convertible securities and/or bonds and money market instruments. Others get the income side of the equation by selling call options on the stocks in their portfolio.

Risk: Moderate

Potential for capital appreciation: Moderate

Potential for current income: Moderate

❑   **Junk-bond funds** invest in the debt of companies that have borrowed heavily and thus need to pay premium interest rates to borrow more. These funds pose greater risks to your principal than traditional fixed-income funds; however, they also typically promise higher rates of return.

Risk: High
Potential for capital appreciation: Low
Potential for current income: High

❑ **Money market funds** invest primarily in short-term government debt, bank deposits, and short-term corporate debt. The net asset values of money market funds are usually pretty stable. However, the yields are also relatively low.

Risk: Very low
Potential for capital appreciation: Very low
Potential for current income: Moderate

❑ **Municipal bond funds** invest primarily in debt issued by state and local governments. Those who buy funds that invest in the debt of their home state are likely to find that the income earned on these accounts is free from both state and federal taxation.

Risk: Moderate
Potential for capital appreciation: Low
Potential for current income: Moderate

❑ **Sector funds** invest in specific industry groups. You would buy a sector fund if, for example, you wanted to participate in the fortunes of just the technology industry, or just the health care industry, or just Net stocks. These funds are highly volatile and relatively undiversified. They are suitable for people who want to take a piece of their assets and gamble a bit.

Risk: Very high
Potential for capital appreciation: Very high
Potential for current income: Very low

Choosing Specific Funds in Each Category

W HEN IT COMES TO CHOOSING SPECIFIC FUNDS IN EACH CATEGORY, YOU HAVE TWO CHOICES: YOU CAN GO WITH so-called index funds, or you can opt for actively managed funds. No matter which you choose, however, you should realize that most mutual funds are going to offer wide diversity with their asset category. So unlike stock investors, who have to pick lots of individual stocks, you can pick just one or two stock funds. The same is true when diversifying your bond or international holdings. If you choose wisely, a fund or two ought to be plenty.

Active versus Passive Management

ACTIVELY MANAGED FUNDS are those in which a portfolio manager aims to beat the overall market's performance by carefully choosing specific investments that the manager believes are primed to excel. The fund manager then actively trades these stocks in an effort to get a better-than-average return.

Index funds, on the other hand, are "passively" managed. They simply aim to mirror the market, not beat it. They do that by buying stocks or bonds that represent the specific investments in a particular market index. For instance, an S&P 500 index fund owns the stocks that make up the Standard and Poor's 500-company stock index. An index fund that aims to mirror the Dow Jones Industrial Average buys stock in the thirty companies that make up the Dow. (Both of these index funds would also fall under the bigger category of growth funds.) The index fund simply holds onto those investments, never trading shares unless the index components change. (Every once in a while, a company that's part of the Dow Thirty, for example, is bought out or goes out of business. At that point, another company is chosen to represent the company that fell out of the index.)

Which is the best way to go? Experts who favor the index approach say that because index funds don't actively trade shares, they generate fewer taxable capital gains. (The gains and losses realized from active trading in a mutual fund are passed on to investors at year-end. If the fund manager has sold stocks at a profit, all the investors in the fund must report—and pay income taxes on—the gains.) Of course, paying less tax as you go along leaves you with more money to invest. More important, while there are always some actively managed funds that handily beat the market at any given time, few beat the averages over long periods. If you are a long-term investor, your odds are better with an index fund. Finally, because there is very little "management" needed to buy and hold stocks that make up an index, annual management fees charged to index fund investors are low. Whereas the average actively managed stock fund may charge 1 percent of the account value in management fees each year, many index funds charge between 0.2 percent and 0.5 percent. The bottom line is that more of the investment return goes to the investor. That, too, has a beneficial effect on the value of your portfolio over time.

Why would anyone buy actively managed funds then? For the same reason that they buy individual stocks. They believe they're capable of using their knowledge about investing to beat the odds. If that describes you, actively managed funds are more your style. Remember, however, that every time you sell shares in an actively managed fund (that's not in a tax-favored retirement account), you'll pay tax on the difference between the fund's net asset value when you sell and its net asset value when you bought it. That reduces the amount you're left with to reinvest, so trade sparingly.

Finding and Researching Funds

NO MATTER whether you want actively or passively managed funds, finding and researching funds has become a snap thanks to the Internet. There are a couple of sites that I find particularly helpful for the individual investor. One is www.mfea.com, which is a site operated by the Mutual Fund Education Alliance. Although the Mutual Fund Education Alliance is particularly interested in low-cost funds—those that don't charge big loads or substantial 12b-1 fees—the site offers information on virtually every fund. You can also sort funds by category and performance and get general information on investing through mutual funds.

If you want some technical analysis of your funds, you can also go to www.morningstar.net. Morningstar Investments of Chicago is one of the nation's premier mutual fund rating services. Funds often advertise their "star" ranking, which is Morningstar's system of giving funds a performance evaluation, ranging from five stars (the best) to one. Morningstar's Web site also allows you to see just how many funds are in a particular fund category and where your fund's performance ranked relative to its peers.

Fund Families

WHEN YOU START TRYING TO PICK AND CHOOSE BETWEEN MUTUAL FUNDS, YOU ARE LIKELY TO FEEL OVERwhelmed. There are thousands of funds to choose from, and the performance of about 75 percent of the industry is pretty good, too. If you try to carefully examine each of your thousands of choices, you'll go crazy—or at least waste a tremendous amount of time that would have been better spent at the park. So how do you narrow your choices to a manageable number?

Look for fund families that offer services that you value. For instance, some fund companies offer twenty-four-hour access to your account via the Web or a toll-free telephone line. Some offer branch offices, where you can go and chat with a fund representative when some life event (or market move) makes you feel uncomfortable and in need of advice. Others may offer low minimum investments, which allow you to invest small amounts at a time—a pivotal feature for somebody who is starting out without a lot of money. Still others may require larger minimum investments but may charge smaller annual management fees, which is an important feature for an investor who has a relatively sizable portfolio and wants to keep costs low.

If you are looking for great convenience, you might also want to limit yourself to big fund families, which can provide you with the ability to keep all your mutual fund investments under one roof. If you're a beginning investor and feel you need lots of helpful reading material about investing, you should also know that some funds are known for their investment literature. They'll send most of it to you for free, although a few funds charge for their more sophisticated investment tools and software.

What are the big fund companies known for?

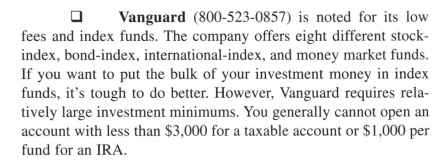

❑ **Vanguard** (800-523-0857) is noted for its low fees and index funds. The company offers eight different stock-index, bond-index, international-index, and money market funds. If you want to put the bulk of your investment money in index funds, it's tough to do better. However, Vanguard requires relatively large investment minimums. You generally cannot open an account with less than $3,000 for a taxable account or $1,000 per fund for an IRA.

❑ **Fidelity Investments** (800-544-8888) is the place to go for vast variety. The company offers roughly 250 different funds, ranging from your basic growth funds to a wide array of sector funds. Some of the company's funds are no-load; others charge either front-end or back-end sales fees. The company also has a handful of branch offices, where you can go to watch the stock ticker or talk to a representative.

❑ **T. Rowe Price** (800-638-5660) offers eighty different no-load funds, ranging from money markets to aggressive stock funds. The company also participates in a fund purchase program called Gateway that allows you to buy about 1,000 other fund companies' funds through T. Rowe. Gateway allows you to get a consolidated statement. In terms of investment minimums, you can either start with a lump sum of $2,500 or, if you don't have that kind of cash in your sock drawer, you can opt for the "systematic purchase option," whereby you simply invest at least $50 a month. (The investment minimum for IRAs is lower— $1,000 as a lump sum or a systematic purchase of at least $50 per month.) T. Rowe is also well known for wonderful investment literature, including brochures on investing for retirement and investing while in retirement.

❑ If you are investing for little nippers, **SteinRoe** (800-338-2550) offers a terrific little fund called the Young Investors Fund. What makes this fund special is that it invests in the stocks of companies that mean something to youthful investors, such as Nike, McDonald's, and Disney, and it produces clever literature—from comic books to quizzes—that explains investing in language kids can understand. The investment minimums vary based on the type of account. However, custodial accounts—those set up on behalf of a minor—generally must be funded with $1,000 or monthly investments of $50 until you reach $1,000; regular taxable accounts usually require a $2,500 lump-sum investment. Meanwhile, you can open an IRA (Roth or traditional) with a minimum investment of $500.

❑ **Janus** (800-525-8983) offers about twenty-one different funds, including domestic and global funds. Minimum investments are $2,500 for a regular account, $500 for an IRA or custodial account. However, if you don't have $2,500 handy, you can start with less ($500) if you promise to fund the account with at least $100 a month until you reach the minimum.

Are there other great fund companies that haven't been mentioned? You bet. Dozens and dozens of them. But these are some of the best and should at least help to get you started on your search.

Selecting a Fund

T O PICK FUNDS THAT WILL WORK NICELY IN YOUR PORT-FOLIO, CONSIDER FIRST HOW YOU LIKE TO INVEST. WHAT services, bells, and whistles are valuable to you? Which are nice but not necessary? Use the following worksheet to guide you.

WORKSHEET
Picking a Fund That Suits You

Contact several mutual fund families to find out whether they offer the services that mean the most to you. If they do, take the next step and ask for details, including the prospectus, of a handful of funds that suit your investment goals.

Here are a few common fund services to jog your memory:

Toll-free telephone access	_____ yes	_____ no
Dividend reinvestment	_____ yes	_____ no
Automatic investment	_____ yes	_____ no
Low investment minimums	_____ yes	_____ no
Convenient branches	_____ yes	_____ no

Informational literature	_____ yes	_____ no
Daily switching	_____ yes	_____ no
Home-computer access	_____ yes	_____ no
Multiple fund choices	_____ yes	_____ no
Other _____	_____ yes	_____ no

Now consider the specifics of individual funds, such as the short- and long-term returns. By looking at the graphs of how a fund has performed, not only can you tell whether shareholders are better off today than when they started, you can also see how badly the fund performed in down markets and how well when times were good. These figures can give you an idea of whether the fund's returns are too lackluster or too volatile for your goals. Realize, however, that a fund that is relatively young may have too short of a track record from which to draw any solid conclusions. Most observers suggest you dismiss long-term information that predates the current fund manager's tenure. For instance, if the fund's very long-term performance is great but the short-term isn't, check to see how long the current fund manager has been managing the fund's assets. If there's a correlation between the two—i.e., the performance fell just as the new manager took over—you know that the long-term returns had little to do with this manager. You may want to scrap this investment, or wait until this manager's track record improves.

If, however, the management has been stable and the average performance has been good, check the year-to-year performance figures to see how volatile the fund is.

Fund's percentage gain in its best year	_____ %
Fund's percentage loss in its worst year	_____ %
Number of years measured	_____

Are the fees reasonable? Take a look at how the fees this fund charges compare with those of similar funds that you're considering. (Be sure you are comparing like funds—i.e., compare domestic stock funds to other domestic stock funds; international funds to other international funds; bond funds to bond funds. Fee structures vary dramatically based on what the fund invests in. Generally speaking, you should expect fees on money market funds to be very low, fees on bond funds to be lower than those on stock funds, and fees on domestic stock funds to be lower than those on international stock funds.) Are they higher, lower, or about the same?

Fees

_____ higher _____ lower _____equivalent

Take a look at the risk section of the proxy. Are all of the risks noted the things you would expect? If not, why not? Now consider whether these are risks you're comfortable taking with your investments.

Risks

_____ acceptable _____unacceptable

The Real Cost of Fund Fees

W HEN HE FIRST STARTED INVESTING, CHARLES ACKEIFI LIKED HIS BROKER SO MUCH THAT HE DIDN'T worry about the price of full-service advice. Sure, a single trade might cost between $75 and $250 versus the $10 to $35 that he would have paid if he employed a discount broker. But Ackeifi liked the idea that his investments were attended by someone who had more time and expertise to devote to his account than he did.

Still, when the brokerage house took a 5 percent fee, called a front-end load, off the top of his index mutual fund investment and then informed him that it would charge a 3 percent annual fee to manage his portfolio of eight stocks—most of which Ackeifi had selected himself—he decided it was time for a change.

"I am upset with the fees they are charging," fumes the forty-two-year-old software consultant from East Grenby, Connecticut. "I think these brokers are out for themselves. Your interests are not paramount."

Although the motivations of full-service brokers certainly can be debated, Ackeifi's story ought to serve as a wake-up call for investors who haven't paid a lot of attention to fees. Fees can make or break an investment. Particularly for those who invest through mutual funds over long periods of time, they can have a dramatic impact on your long-term wealth. Consider that if Ackeifi invested $100,000 in a high-cost S&P 500 index fund—one with a 5 percent load and 0.5 percent in annual expenses—and maintained that investment for twenty years, he would pay $68,197 more in total costs than if he invested in a similar no-load index fund that charges only 0.2 percent in annual expenses.

Fees, of course, are not the only consideration when choosing a fund. However, when comparing several similar funds, fees should be an important part of the equation. Yet many investors don't compare the cost of funds this carefully, partly because it's difficult. That's largely because mutual fund fees come in great variety. As noted earlier in this chapter, every fund charges annual management fees, for instance, but some also charge annual marketing levies called 12b-1 fees. Some charge up-front fees, called front-end loads, or fees when you sell, called back-end loads. Some give you the option of choosing one fee structure over the other. For instance, investors might be presented with a choice of a front-end load, a back-end load, or a 12b-1 fee. Unless you are very skilled with a calculator, it's difficult to make the comparison.

On the bright side, if you have a computer and Web access, the Securities and Exchange Commission (SEC) will help you do the math. The agency has posted a "mutual fund cost calculator" on

147

its Web site, www.sec.gov. When you get to the site, click on "Investor Assistance and Complaints," then look for the box labeled "SEC News You Can Use." You can download the file and use it to make apples-to-apples comparisons of the cost of buying funds that have orange-and-lemon-like fee structures.

This calculator allows you to figure the total cost of investing in a fund—adding in the cost of loads, if any, 12b-1 fees, annual management fees, and the like—over the entire time you expect to own the fund. The amount of time you expect to own the fund is important when comparing fees because certain fee structures are expensive at first but become less so over time. Meanwhile, other types of fees that may appear innocuous can rob you of solid long-term performance.

For instance, let's say you want to figure out whether it makes more sense to buy fund ABC, which charges a 5 percent load and 1 percent in annual management fees, or a similar no-load fund, XYZ, that charges 2 percent in annual management and 12b-1 fees. Just for example's sake, we'll say that you have $100,000 to invest in either fund. By using the SEC calculator, you can see that the better choice hinges on whether you plan to own the fund for two years or twenty. If you plan to hold this investment for just two years, the front-loaded ABC fund will cost you nearly twice as much—$8,337.51 versus $4,792 for XYZ. But if you're going to own this fund for twenty years, ABC is significantly less expensive, costing $150,015 versus $223,617 for XYZ. Over thirty years, XYZ will cost you a quarter of a million dollars more than ABC. Why? That insidious extra 1 percent in annual expenses eats up a tremendous amount of your return over time.

Notably, these numbers are higher than the raw amount of fees that you would get if you simply added the amount you expect to pay in fees year after year. That's because the SEC calculator takes into account foregone earnings. In essence it accounts for the fact that the money you paid out in fees in year one was not there to earn a return for you in year two. That's a significant cost.

chapter 9

Socially Responsible Investing

I N THE BEGINNING, there was a guiding principle: Thou shalt not make money from industries that do harm.

From this sprang a small cadre of so-called ethical investors. Primarily well-heeled religious folk, ethical investors followed their creed by sidestepping investments in tobacco, alcohol, and gambling companies. In the 1960s and 1970s—during the Vietnam War—the movement expanded to add agents of war, such as manufacturers of guns, bombers, and nuclear weaponry, to the list of shalt-nots. And they quietly invested, secure in the knowledge that even though they couldn't change the world, ethical investors would at least sleep knowing that their money was not being used to do harm.

Evolving Influence

A CRY FOR HELP CHANGED EVERYTHING. IN THE EARLY 1980s, BISHOPS OF THE ANGLICAN CHURCH IN SOUTH Africa appealed to their brethren in the American Episcopal Church to help them end apartheid. When a decade of quiet urging proved fruitless, the ethical investors got more boisterous and started enlisting powerful allies, including managers of multibillion-dollar pension funds and city and state treasurers.

When they flexed their collective muscle by divesting themselves of investments in companies doing business in South Africa, that country's economy went into a tailspin. Suddenly, South Africa's white minority government sat down to bargain with the black majority, which helped lead to a complete change in the system of government. And it also changed this segment of the investing world forever.

"It was a watershed period," says Amy Domini, author of several books on the topic and founder of Domini Social Investments in New York. "Until then, we called ourselves 'ethical' investors because we didn't want to imply that what we were doing was going to make a difference. It turned out that we could be part of the solution."

Little more than a decade later, ethical investing has been renamed socially responsible investing to reflect the industry's newfound power and tactics. Now, instead of sidestepping companies with questionable track records, some social funds invest in these companies to press for change. They're not just looking at "sin" stocks anymore either. They're involved in an array of environmental and employee-relations issues, from sustainable logging to sweatshops and the treatment of women in the workplace.

Promising Performance

THE LONG-HELD BELIEF THAT INVESTING WITH YOUR HEART WILL PINCH YOUR POCKETBOOK HAS PROVED A myth. A recent study by the Washington, D.C.–based Social Investment Forum found that 70 percent of the nation's largest socially screened mutual funds outperformed their nonscreened peers in 1998.

"The thought was that if you invested socially, you sacrificed return. But in fact you can win, lose, or draw, just like anyone else," says Tim Grant, president of the Pax World Fund family in New York, which uses social screens. "We've gotten a market return. There are some funds that are winning, some are losing, and some are in the middle."

Adds J. B. Miller, national sales manager for the MMA-Praxis mutual funds, "Our portfolio managers say that poor performance is not a result of the social screens; it's a function of poor stock selection."

And Domini Social Equity Fund, an index fund of 400 companies that have passed social screens relating to their lines of business and their employment practices, beat the Standard and Poor's 500 index in one-year, three-year, five-year, and since-inception (1991) returns, through 1998's first quarter. That's a feat few other funds—socially screened or not—can meet.

The social-investment movement is growing rapidly. From 1995 to 1997, assets in socially screened portfolios surged 227 percent, to $529 billion from $162 billion, according to the Social

Investment Forum.

But individual investors who want to get involved in social investing might want to do a little soul-searching first, Miller says: "I would ask myself, 'What are those things that I value?' Are there things that you would feel totally uncomfortable with if you found them in your portfolio?" You then need to consider whether your ethical and social concerns are addressed by a mutual fund or whether your concerns are so specific that you ought to invest in individual companies.

Social Fund Screens

ALMOST ALL SOCIAL FUNDS SCREEN OUT INVESTMENTS IN "SIN" STOCKS—COMPANIES THAT PRODUCE AND SELL alcohol and tobacco or facilitate gambling. Most also avoid defense contractors and gun manufacturers. Some avoid the purveyors of nuclear power. Many use "positive screens" to buy into companies that appear to have progressive work practices or particularly good environmental records. However, only a small number have looked at other tricky issues, such as animal testing. And their positions on issues such as the environment, for example, can vary.

There is, however, now nearly universal agreement that social investing can make a difference. "We know that we are not going to completely change a company's behavior or product line," Miller says. "We are not going to buy shares in a tobacco company and try to get them out of the tobacco business. But we do believe we can help shape a company's behavior—at least along the edges. We can encourage them to be good corporate citizens and good employers. We are in this because we truly believe we have a role to play."

Domini says her view on the movement's impact is summed up by a fable that is reflected in the company's logo—and virtually everything it does:

Thousands of starfish washed ashore.

A little girl began throwing them back in the water so they wouldn't die.

Don't bother, dear," her mother said. "It won't make a difference."

The little girl stopped for a moment and looked at the starfish in her hand. "It will make a difference to this one," she said.

Finding Mutual Funds with a Socially Responsible Bent

T HINK YOU'RE READY TO PUT YOUR MONEY WHERE YOUR VALUES ARE? THE TOUGHEST PART OF SO-CALLED SOCIAL investing has always been finding the companies and funds that have values that match yours. However, this process has recently been made easier thanks to several resources that are now available on the World Wide Web.

For instance, www.socialinvest.org, the Social Investment Forum, a Washington, D.C.–based nonprofit, provides information about what social investing is all about and where you can go to find investments that suit your needs. This site concentrates on mutual funds that screen out investments in certain types of companies. Your job is to determine the types of investments you want to avoid and then match your concerns to a fund that has similar goals.

For instance, if the environment is your primary concern, you'd want to make sure that you don't invest in companies that are major polluters or destroyers of the rain forest or the ozone layer. If social-equity issues are your bag, you'd want to avoid companies that employ sweatshop laborers or have discriminatory hiring practices. Hate war? There are funds that won't invest in defense contractors and weapons manufacturers. There are also screens for so-called sin stocks—those of companies that manufacture or promote alcohol, tobacco, and gambling— and a few for companies that do animal testing.

In fact, if you click on "mutual funds chart" on the Social Investment Forum's home page, you'll flip to a page that lists socially screened funds by investment category—i.e., domestic stock, bonds, international, balanced funds, and money markets. Next to each fund listing, the chart notes which of seven common social screens—environment, labor/employment, products/services, defense/weapons, "sins" (alcohol, tobacco, gambling), animal testing, and human rights/equality issues—that fund uses to direct its investment philosophy. (The listing also shows minimum deposit requirements and toll-free phone numbers for the various funds.)

Clearly the chart doesn't provide enough detail on the funds' philosophies, social criteria, and investment performance to make it one-stop shopping. However, it gives investors the ability to winnow down their list of possibilities to a few before researching further.

A second chart helps investors ferret out the best performers among socially screened funds. This alphabetical listing of social funds (www.socialinvest.org/Areas/SRIguide/mfpc.asp) tells when the funds were started and how much they hold in assets and provides their average annual performance based on one-year, three-year, five-year, ten-year, and since-inception time periods. The chart also indicates whether the funds have a load— an up-front fee charged as a percentage of the amount invested— and lists the funds' annual expense ratio.

Naturally, serious investors will want to know more, such as year-by-year performance and information about fund managers and risks. But in most cases that information is only a click away.

The site offers links to the home pages of the vast majority of funds listed. Click on the fund you're interested in, and you zoom through cyberspace to another Web page that provides more detailed information.

What if you're not wired to the Web? There's an inexpensive, low-tech version, called the *National Green Pages*, which is a listing of some 2,000 socially and environmentally screened businesses, including banks, mutual funds, and financial planners. The guide costs $10.95 including shipping and handling. You can order the guide through Co-op America, a Washington, D.C. nonprofit, by phone or mail: Co op America, 1612 K Street NW, Washington, D.C. 20006; 800-58-GREEN (800-584-7336).

chapter 10

International Investing

THE FOREIGN LABELS on the things you buy should signal two things to you as an investor: One, to maintain your current buying power, you need a certain amount of international exposure. Two, there are some great companies producing world-class products overseas. That spells opportunity.

"It used to be that the United States dominated the world economy, so it was appropriate for U.S. investors to ignore the rest of the world," says James J. Atkinson Jr., director of Guinness Flight Global Asset Management

Ltd. in Pasadena, California. "But you can't make that claim anymore."

Indeed, though the U.S. stock market remains the biggest in the world, foreign markets now account for about 50 percent of the world's stock market capitalization. Concentrating all your dollars in the domestic markets means you are ignoring half of the world's investment opportunities.

"We are in an environment of global companies, global distribution, and global consumerism," says Mark Geist, president of Montgomery Asset Management in San Francisco. "Every investor should have a portion of their portfolio invested globally, too."

Effect on Diversified Portfolios

W HAT MAY BE THE MOST COMPELLING REASON OF ALL TO INVEST IN FOREIGN MARKETS IS THIS: A HOST OF INDEpendent studies suggest that international investments have had an unusual effect on diversified portfolios. They reduced overall risk and modestly increased the potential return, according to Ibbotson Associates in Chicago. Ibbotson has tracked a historical link between the performance of U.S. and foreign stock markets. The two markets are not closely correlated. In other words, when U.S. stocks are rising, foreign stocks could be falling, and vice versa.

Because the markets can move at different times and different speeds, foreign stocks can smooth out the bumps in your domestic portfolio. That does more than save you money on antacids. It actually improves your portfolio's overall performance over time. Even as world economies become more interdependent and interrelated, many analysts think this state of affairs is likely to continue. But even the biggest advocates of foreign investments agree that they are best taken in moderation, because many foreign markets are more volatile than U.S. markets. In addition, currency risk can magnify these swings.

What's currency risk? All world currencies, whether U.S. dollars, French francs, Japanese yen, or German marks (or the Euro—the new currency of many European countries), fluctuate in value when measured against one another. When you buy stock in a foreign company, you normally buy the shares with that country's currency, after converting dollars to the currency at that day's exchange rate. When you sell, you get paid in that country's currency, and you then must convert it back to dollars at the going exchange rate.

Exchange Rate Implications

I F THE EXCHANGE RATE IS SIGNIFICANTLY DIFFERENT BETWEEN THE TIME YOU BUY AND THE TIME YOU SELL, IT can either add to or reduce whatever return you earned on the stock itself. In some cases, the change in currency values can be more significant to your total return than the actual appreciation or depreciation of the particular stocks you purchased.

If the dollar weakens in value against another currency, you make money on the currency exchange, because each unit of foreign currency translates into more dollars. If the dollar strengthens against another currency, you lose on the currency exchange, because each unit of foreign currency translates into fewer dollars.

To illustrate, consider a hypothetical individual, John, who invested $10,000 in Japanese stocks in April 1995—a time when the Japanese yen was at record strength against the dollar—and sold them in October 1996.

When John bought, his $10,000 was converted into 843,000 yen worth of stocks, because $1 equaled 84.3 yen at the time. In yen terms, his stocks appreciated a solid 20 percent over the period as the market rose, making the securities worth 1,011,600 yen when he sold.

But in the same time period, the dollar strengthened considerably against the yen. Instead of 84.3 yen needed to equal $1, it took 114 yen to equal $1 when John sold. So after converting his yen to dollars, John came home with just $8,874—a $1,126 loss, caused solely by currency swings.

On the other hand, a U.S. investor who bought Japanese stocks in 1990 and made no return on the stocks at all would have earned a tidy amount when converting Japanese currency back to dollars, because the dollar's value has weakened considerably against the yen over that time. Where $1 bought 140 yen in 1990, it bought about 104 yen at the beginning of 2000.

Currency risk isn't the only worry for Americans investing abroad. Investing directly in international markets can be prohibitively expensive and inconvenient if you try to do it alone. Fees are high, some stocks cannot be sold quickly, and there are many delays in transferring funds. This is particularly true of the smaller stock markets in less-developed nations.

Of course, it is possible to buy some foreign stocks on U.S. exchanges. Such issues trade as American Depositary Receipts (ADRs) and are quoted in dollars. Although it is increasing, the number of such stocks is still limited.

International Mutual Funds and Related Investment Vehicles

F OR THE MOST PART, THE SIMPLEST AND MOST ECONOMI-CAL WAY TO INVEST IN INTERNATIONAL MARKETS IS through mutual funds. Although fund companies also must pay the brokerage settlement and exchange fees involved, they're able to get better rates because they are buying in bulk. The costs are also spread among a larger group of investors.

International mutual funds are not all alike. Some invest in single foreign markets, others invest in specific regions (such as the Pacific Rim), and others invest all over the world. Some try to hedge away currency risk, while others embrace it. Then, too, some funds take a top-down approach to stock picking, choosing the countries first and the specific stocks second, while others pick the stocks of companies they like no matter what country the company is based in. By and large, these differences are clearly delineated in each fund's prospectus (see Chapter 8, on mutual funds), a detailed legal document provided to investors that spells out the fund's risks, strategies, fees, and historical returns.

Savvy investors analyze whether a fund's investment strategy meshes nicely with their own. Consider, for example, whether you want your fund to bank on one country's economic strength or if you'd prefer a fund that has a broader reach. Does currency risk make you cringe, or can you handle extra risk with the potential for better rewards? Do you want to invest in so-called emerging markets—less-developed countries, where stocks may experience tremendous volatility over the short run but could provide more generous returns over long time periods? Or are you more comfortable investing in mature economies with track records—the Germanys and Japans of the world—because their markets tend to be more predictable?

Another option is so-called global funds, which differ from international funds in that they have the flexibility to invest a substantial portion of their assets in the U.S. market when fund managers think that's where the best opportunities lie. International funds, on the other hand, are generally required to invest the bulk of their assets overseas.

Foreign stocks also can be purchased via "closed-end" funds. Unlike open-end mutual funds, closed-end funds raise capital once and invest it. Their shares, which trade on major exchanges, can sell at a discount or premium to the true value of the underlying portfolio.

After you decide which type of fund is best for you, the only question is how much money you want to invest overseas. There's no pat answer, but experts advise individuals to dedicate anywhere from 5 percent to 25 percent of their portfolios to international investments. The more time you have, the more exposure you can handle in volatile—but potentially rewarding—foreign markets.

The 'Buy American' Approach to Foreign Investment

T HANKS TO THE U.S. MARKET'S RELENTLESS AND RECORD-BREAKING PERFORMANCE IN RECENT YEARS, there are a number of investors who say that you may not need international diversification at all. After all, diversifying into markets that aren't performing as well as your own is sure to depress your overall returns. What about reducing the risk in your portfolio by moving some assets into markets that rise and fall at different times? These pundits argue that because big U.S. companies often have operations overseas, you can diversify internationally by doing nothing fancier than buying shares in Coca-Cola and General Electric.

Admittedly, those who had done just that between 1996 and 1999 would have done far better than the intrepid investor who stepped into the international markets. Between currency crises and economic and political scandals and upheaval, one market after the next has toppled, while residents in these countries suffered crippling inflation and diminished living standards. Investors, particularly those who participated in the recent declines of the once-bright stars of Latin America and Southeast Asia, are understandably gun-shy.

Still, if you're able to talk yourself into taking some of your profits out of U.S. stocks and putting the money into depressed foreign markets, you would be following age-old wisdom: "Buy low, sell high." The strategy makes long-term sense, because no one can predict when any market is ready to soar or slump. Indeed, the herd mentality is often wrong.

"If you got out of America when it was popular [in the 1960s, when U.S. stocks were rising much like they did throughout the 1990s] and into Japan when it was unpopular [around the same time], you would have made a fortune," says Thomas S. White Jr., president of Thomas White Funds and manager of the Thomas White International Fund in Chicago. "But it doesn't feel comfortable, because you think you know which country is going to do best. Then everybody thought that Japan was perfect in 1989. They did everything right; we [the U.S.] did everything wrong. Then they had a bear market for ten years."

Of course, such a move requires fortitude on the part of investors. Going against the crowd means you must be confident enough to handle the ridicule of your friends (or even the cocktail-party guy). On the bright side, fundamental economic indicators suggest that such fortitude will pay off over time.

Consider how the value of various countries' stock markets contrasted with the goods and services that these economies actually produced—two figures that in theory, at least, should move more or less in tandem, since stock prices follow corporate earnings. In marketspeak, this compares market capitalization (the value of all of the stocks trading on a particular exchange) to that country's share of global gross domestic product (a measurement of all of the goods and services a country produces). U.S. equities accounted for more than 50 percent of the value of every stock trading on every exchange in the world in 1999. But U.S. companies produced less than 30 percent of the goods and services bought and sold around the world.

By contrast, Japan, which went through a decade of slumping stock prices, produced about 14 percent of the goods the world consumed in 1999, but the value of companies traded on Japan's stock exchange accounted for less than 8 percent of the global market value.

This comparison was reversed a decade ago. In 1988, Japanese stocks accounted for 40 percent of the value of the world's corporate shares, while the country produced less than 20 percent of the goods and services consumed around the globe. At the same time, U.S. stock values and its domestic product were nearly in sync.

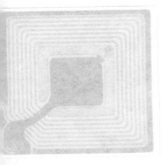

A Graphic Look at Currency Risk

J ANE SMITH DECIDES SHE WANTS TO GET INTO THE FOR-EIGN STOCK MARKETS. SHE BUYS $1,000 IN MEXICAN stocks and $1,000 in German stocks at a time when each U.S. dollar buys one Mexican peso and one German mark. The value of the shares she purchased rises 10 percent over the course of the year in both countries. However, because Jane must bring the proceeds back into the United States to spend the money, her final return will hinge on just how many marks and pesos will be required to buy a dollar. In this case, let's say the value of the Mexican peso dropped, so it now takes 1.3 pesos to buy a dollar. Meanwhile, the value of the German mark rose, so it takes just 0.9 marks to buy a dollar.

Investments	Mexican	German
Purchase price	$1,000	$1,000
Appreciation	+$100	+$100
Proceeds from sale (in foreign currency)	$1,100	$1,100
Divided by the cost of a U.S. dollar	÷1.30	÷0.90
Net proceeds in U.S. dollars	$846	$1,222
Total return	-15.4%	+22.2%

chapter 11

Tax-Favored Investing

T HE TAX TAIL should never wag the investment dog. You know that this saying remains true. And yet if you can get the dog and the tail going in the same direction at the same time, you may have the best of both worlds—a good return that you get to keep.

"It probably shouldn't be your No. 1 investment criterion, but [taxes] ought to be in your top three or four," says Philip J. Holthouse, partner at the Los Angeles tax law and accounting firm Holthouse Carlin & Van Trigt. "If you don't take the tax consequences into account, you are cheating yourself."

There are plenty of opportunities to combine investing and tax management in profitable ways. But the increasing array of choices is making the process complicated for the average investor. And that can lead to costly mistakes.

Holthouse has seen dozens of them. He's had clients—sophisticated, high-income types—fail to realize that they triggered taxable gains when they sold one mutual fund and bought another within the same fund family. He's seen high-income individuals sell a stock one month too soon—within eleven months of the purchase, which precludes them from claiming preferential capital gains tax rates on the profit. Their federal tax hit jumps to about 40 percent from 20 percent on the transaction. He's seen people put variable annuities and municipal bonds in retirement accounts—an unnecessary and costly doubling up of tax-favored vehicles.

Worse still, he's seen individuals pull money out of retirement plans to pay off bills or buy luxury items. The hit—taxes and penalties—is crushing, usually about half of the amount withdrawn, and these individuals forever lose the benefit of allowing that money to grow for long periods on a tax-favored basis.

So what are the wise ways to minimize the taxes on your investments?

❑ **Invest in tax-managed accounts.** Mutual fund companies are increasingly offering funds that promise to manage the taxable income passed on to you. One of the more effective strategies they use is simply not to trade shares often. Index funds, which buy and hold all the stocks in a particular index, are among the most tax-efficient. Generally the only gains they pass on to investors are dividends and an occasional long-term gain from selling shares in a company that's been bought out or has otherwise fallen out of the index.

❑ **Trade sparingly.** The best way to manage your capital gains bills is not to trigger any gains. After all, you have to pay capital gains taxes only if you sell shares at a profit. If you buy stocks because you think the company has great long-term potential, and nothing dramatic has occurred to make you change your mind, sit tight.

❑ **If you must trade, trade in tax-favored accounts.** There are options galore—Roth IRAs, traditional IRAs, Keogh accounts, and 401(k)s, for instance—that shelter your gains from tax until you pull the money out at retirement. The first three types of accounts allow you to completely self-direct your investments. (You also self-direct your investments with a 401(k), but your options are usually more limited.) You can buy individual stocks, mutual funds, bonds, certificates of deposit, and so on. And if you decide you want to alter your investment mix, you can sell any or all of your holdings without triggering a taxable gain. Of course, you also can't use capital losses realized within a retirement account when figuring your taxes. So do your best to trade wisely.

❑ **Fully fund any tax-favored account you have available.** Start with your 401(k) at work. Contributions to 401(k) plans and similar plans, such as 403(b) plans for teachers and 457 plans for other government employees, are deducted from your taxable income, so they reduce your federal income tax when you contribute. Additionally, most employers match anywhere from 25 percent to 100 percent of their workers' 401(k) contributions, up to set amounts. So if you put in $100, the employer kicks in an additional, say, $50. You make a 50 percent return on your money before you've invested a dime. You don't pay current income tax on either the company contributions or the investment income you've earned on the account, either. It grows and compounds on a tax-deferred basis until you withdraw the money. It doesn't get much better than that.

What if you have a 401(k) at work but have not been contributing to it because you want to pay off your debts first? You may be giving up more than you know. Let's say you're in the 28 percent federal tax bracket, like most working Americans. If you contribute $5,000 annually to a 401(k), or $417 per month, that reduces your taxable income by the same amount. The result is that you pay $1,400 less in federal income tax that year. Or to put it another way, your $5,000 contribution has a net cost to you of $3,600. Now your employer kicks in, say, 25 percent, or an additional $1,250 a year ($104 per month). Then you earn an average of 10 percent on your money. At the end of year one, you have $6,545. Considering that your net (after-tax) cost was $3,600, that's an 82 percent return. That beats the 20 percent interest savings you would get by paying off your credit-card debt by a wide margin.

But if you want to be really smart, figure that you have $5,000 annually to spend. Because a $5,000 401(k) contribution is going to cost you only $3,600 after tax, use the remaining $1,400 to pay down your debt. Keep it up, and you would pay off your $5,000 debt in less than five years. Your 401(k), assuming you keep earning that average annual return of 10 percent, will be worth a tidy $40,332.

What about buying variable annuities and municipal bonds? If you are very wealthy—paying income taxes at the nation's highest rates—municipal bonds can make sense for a good part of the fixed-income portion of your portfolio. Unfortunately, many people with scant taxable income buy munis so they don't have to pay income tax on the investment income. But because municipals generally pay significantly less interest than taxable bonds, these people often get a lower after-tax return than they'd earn on a taxable-bond investment.

As for variable annuities, they work for high-income individuals who have maximized their other tax-favored retirement account options but still want to save more. But they're a sorry substitute for investing in a 401(k). And some tax advisers argue that they're less attractive than simply investing in stocks or tax-managed mutual funds for the long term. Annuities are less flexible than taxable investments, these advisers note. And when you permanently withdraw money from an annuity, your investment gains are taxable at ordinary income tax rates rather than at the lower capital gains rates.

Running the Numbers: Details on Tax-Favored versus Taxable

H OW MUCH OF A DIFFERENCE DOES TAX-FAVORED INVEST-ING MAKE? FRANKLY, THE PRECISE FIGURE DEPENDS ON a variety of variables that are impossible to predict accurately— such as your tax rate at retirement and the rate of return you'll earn on your money each year. But making a few guesses and running them through an example or two can help illustrate.

Consider an investor, Sam Smart, who puts $100 a month into mutual funds in his company's 401(k) plan—a tax-deferred retirement account—and earns 10 percent on average annually over a forty-year period. At retirement, he has $632,408.

His friend, Sue Savvy, invests in a taxable mutual fund instead and pays income tax from her fund account each year. Even though Savvy invests the same amount and earns the same investment return as Smart, she accumulates much less—just $349,101. (To simplify matters, we've assumed that the fund has realized 100 percent of its capital gains, and she pays federal income tax on all of it at a 20 percent rate. In reality, most mutual funds would defer at least some gains, and individual tax consequences can vary.)

When Savvy retires, she doesn't have to worry much about taxes. Smart, on the other hand, must pay tax on the 401(k) when he withdraws the money at retirement. If he takes the money out in one lump sum, he'll push himself into the highest marginal tax bracket, but he'll still end up with about $380,000 after surrendering 39.6 percent of his savings in federal income taxes.

If, in a more likely scenario, he takes money out over time, the money withdrawn from the 401(k) will be taxed at a more modest rate. In any event, Smart is somewhere between $30,000 and $100,000 (depending on his tax rate at retirement) richer than Savvy simply because he was able to collect investment returns—and allow them to compound year after year—on money that otherwise would have been paid to the government.

Which is all to say, tax-favored compounding is a powerful force. Just how powerful it will be depends on other considerations. Tax rates that are much higher at retirement will reduce Sam Smart's advantage, while lower tax rates at retirement could cause his advantage to multiply. Unrelated capital losses might reduce the taxes on gains Sue Savvy would pay along the way. And tax law changes are, of course, unpredictable.

Major Options

ERE ARE THE PROS AND CONS OF THE MAJOR OPTIONS FOR TAX-DEFERRED INVESTING—RETIREMENT ACCOUNTS, annuities, and growth stocks—and the pros and cons of municipal bonds, which offer outright tax avoidance on the interest.

Retirement Accounts

GENERALLY SPEAKING, traditional retirement accounts (this excludes the Roth IRA) have two major advantages. Contributions are tax-deductible, so, as an incentive for saving, you pay less current income tax. In addition, investment income earned in your retirement account is not taxed until you start to withdraw it.

But there are two major disadvantages: When you withdraw the money, every dollar—including your principal—counts as taxable income (assuming you took the deductions up front as you contributed). And withdrawals are taxable at your ordinary income tax rate, which may be higher than the capital gains rates that might otherwise apply to long-term investment gains.

In addition, if you take your money out before retirement, you'll get hit with penalties—hefty ones. The federal government generally imposes a 10 percent tax penalty on retirement funds withdrawn before age fifty-nine and a half. And many states impose their own penalties besides. California, for example, imposes a penalty amounting to 2.5 percent of the withdrawn amount.

A variety of tax-deferred retirement accounts are offered to different groups of people and are subject to different rules and regulations. For example, there are Keogh plans for self-employed individuals; traditional individual retirement accounts; Roth IRAs, which don't offer up-front deductions but promise tax-free withdrawals; 403(b) plans for teachers and employees of nonprofit organizations; and so-called 457 plans for government workers.

❑   **401(k) plans.** These are one of the more flexible and attractive retirement plans around. The vast majority of large employers offer these company-sponsored retirement programs. In 2001 they allowed workers to set aside up to $10,500 of their wages annually if their company program rules allow it and to deduct this amount from their taxable earnings. Someone contributing $10,500 would reduce his or her annual tax bite by $2,940 if that person was in the 28 percent federal tax bracket. (This person would save on state income taxes, too.)

Investment options for contributed savings differ by plan, but generally you are able to choose among company stock, mutual fund, and simple savings accounts. Investment gains and dividend income that accumulate in the account are also exempt from income tax until the money is withdrawn.

But what really differentiates these accounts from other tax-favored investment options is that most employers match worker contributions, kicking in $.25 to $.50 for every $1 the employee saves. That supercharges the returns, making it far easier to save a substantial sum.

Equally attractive is the fact that many companies allow workers to borrow as much as $50,000 or 50 percent of their 401(k) savings, whichever is less, to finance anything from a home purchase to a college education. This reduces the need to make actual withdrawals (which would incur penalties). Other retirement plans don't offer savers this kind of flexibility.

❑ **Roth IRAs**. These retirement accounts don't offer up-front tax deductions, but they promise big tax breaks in the end. The way they work is this: Qualifying individuals can contribute up to $2,000 per year. Your contributions are not tax deductible, but if you leave your money alone for at least five years and then withdraw only for a "qualified purpose," such as retirement, death, disability, or to make a "qualified first-time home-buyer purchase," all the money you take out—principal and interest—is tax free.

There are, however, some restrictions. Your ability to contribute to a Roth IRA is limited if you earn more than $95,000 when single or more than $150,000 when married. Once your income exceeds $110,000 when single or $160,000 when married, your ability to contribute phases out completely.

However, if you meet all the restrictions and have a very long time to save, Roths can be tremendously powerful tools. For example, if a twenty-year-old woman started saving $2,000 a year and kept it up for ten years, then left the money alone until she retired at age sixty-five, how much money would she have? She would have saved a total of $20,000 of her own money, but at an average 10 percent annual return on her investment, she would have accumulated a stunning $1.1 million at retirement. If that money was in an ordinary retirement account, it would all be taxable at her ordinary income tax rate. Assuming that she paid tax at 28 percent, that would cost her about $300,000 in federal income tax. But if it were in a Roth, none of that tax would be due.

❑ **Traditional IRAs.** It's worth mentioning that if you qualify to make contributions to either a traditional IRA or a Roth, the traditional IRA is worth careful consideration. That's because you get tax deductions today, as well as the benefit of tax-deferred earnings within the account. When you pull the money out at retirement, it is taxable at your ordinary income tax rates. But if your time horizon is fairly short—fifteen years or less—or if your investment strategy is conservative, causing you to accumulate less investment earnings in your account, the up-front tax benefits of the traditional IRA can prove more compelling than the back-end benefits of the Roth. If you'd like to compare your options, there are dozens of calculators on the Web that allow you to plug in your numbers and see how the two IRAs compare. You can find one such calculator at www.fidelity.com/ira.

Tax-Deferred Annuities

LIKE STANDARD RETIREMENT ACCOUNTS, annuities are essentially "shells" through which you can invest in securities such as stocks and bonds, deferring taxes on earnings until you begin withdrawing the money at retirement.

But unlike standard retirement accounts, the money you contribute to an annuity is not tax-deductible. What's more, if you pull money out before retirement, you'll get hit with federal and state tax penalties. If you pull the money out before your annuity contract allows it, you may also get hit with a so-called surrender fee from the insurer.

On the bright side, annuities get their special tax treatment because they're "wrapped" with a life insurance policy. By and large, that insurance policy guarantees only one thing: If you die and the market crashes at the same time, the insurer will make sure your heirs get at least as much as you contributed to your account. But the cost of the insurance policy boosts the annual fees imposed on your annuity account, and that depresses your total return.

Growth Stocks

ANOTHER TAX-FAVORED investment alternative is to buy and hold stock in companies that grow and appreciate. What will that get you? Until you sell, you won't have to pay tax on the stock's price appreciation.

Let's say you put $100 a month into the stock of a fast-growing company, and the stock appreciates 10 percent a year on average. At the end of the fortieth year, you have $632,408 in stock— just as much as Sam Smart has in his 401(k). But Sam pays taxes on his 401(k) at ordinary income tax rates. And he pays tax on the entire amount in the account. You, on the other hand, are going to pay tax at a 20 percent capital gains rate, and only on the appreciation, not on the principal. Subtracting your principal investment of $48,000 made over the forty years, if you sold your stock worth $632,408, you'd pay $116,882 in federal capital gains taxes, leaving you with $575,526.

That's more than Sam Smart ends up with, unless he is in a very low tax bracket at retirement. And if you end up leaving money to charity or heirs, there are significant tax advantages to giving appreciated stock rather than trying to give away 401(k) funds. On the other hand, Smart got up-front tax deductions that you didn't get when investing directly in stocks. And if he got matching funds from his employer, he's probably ahead.

Municipal Bonds

THESE BONDS, which are debt issued by cities, states, and counties, pay interest that is tax free to residents of the state in which the bonds are issued. If you are in the highest federal and state tax brackets, municipal bonds can be a good bet. Although they pay relatively low rates of interest, all the interest earnings are free from federal and state income taxes.

chapter 12

Starting Small

T HINK YOU'RE TOO POOR to invest in stocks? Many people do, partly because they know that most brokerage firms and mutual funds require at least $1,000 or $2,000 to even open an account. However, there are several ways that you can get started with as little as $25 to $50 a month. Better yet, new opportunities are arising daily, thanks to cheap online trading services, which are increasingly accommodating to individual investors who don't have a lot of cash.

In 1999, for example, two companies—Netstock Direct

Corp. and BUYandHOLD.com Inc.—launched online trading services that let individuals invest as little as $10 or $20 a month in stocks. There are no other investment minimums. Trading fees generally range from $2 to $2.99.

If the amount you've chosen to invest won't buy you a full share of stock, these companies will buy you a fractional share. In other words, if you can afford to invest just $20 a month but want to buy stock in a company that sells for $60 per share, they'll buy you roughly one-third of a share each month.

The downside is that neither Netstock nor BUYandHOLD offers "real-time" trading. Netstock buys shares once or twice weekly; BUYandHOLD promises to buy twice a day. The same is true for sales. (Netstock will offer investors the option of selling in real time, but the cost is higher: $19.95 per trade.)

Still, if you are a long-term investor looking for a way to accumulate shares, being able to trade in the blink of an eye isn't a huge issue. At the same time, the ability to trade in small amounts gives virtually any working American the chance to start investing—no matter how little he or she earns.

How much of a nest egg can you accumulate with these small regular investments? If you save just $20 a month and earn 10 percent on your money, you could have $45,210 socked away in thirty years. If you save $25 a month, earning the same 10 percent on average, you'd have $56,512; $30 a month would generate $67,815 in savings; and $40 a month would net you $90,420. You can save $50 a month, you say? Great. You'll have more than $113,000 in thirty years, assuming you earn an average annual return of 10 percent on your money.

Other Options
for Small Investments

N OTABLY, THE SERVICES OFFERED BY NETSTOCK AND BUYANDHOLD ARE ONLY THE LATEST OFFERINGS IN A wide array of options available to those who don't have a lot of money to invest. Many mutual fund companies also allow you to make small monthly investments. However, they generally require investments of at least $50 per month.

Additionally, you can participate in so-called direct stock purchase programs that are now offered by more than 1,000 companies nationwide. Direct stock purchase plans often allow you to buy stock in the company of your choice without paying any brokerage fees at all.

Specifically, what are your options if you want or need to start small? **Netstock Direct's** individual investor program is called Sharebuilder. You can sign up or learn more online at www.sharebuilder.com. The way the program works is this: You set up an account. During this process, you'll be asked how much you want to invest and how you'll pay for those investments. Netstock will require that your investments be made through an automatic debit from your checking or savings account. You'll also get to choose which company's shares to buy from a list of more than 200 companies. If a company you want is not on the list, you can e-mail Netstock. The company's president, Jeff Seely, says the firm adds additional companies when there is demand for them.

Each time you buy stock through Netstock, you'll be charged a $2 trading fee. Your shares will be purchased sometime during the week that your account is debited. (There's a discount if the account is for a minor, however. Minors' accounts are charged just $1 per stock purchase.)

To set up an account with **BUYandHOLD**, you must send the brokerage company a check. However, after that, you can arrange to make subsequent investments through automatic investments or by sending the company more checks. The day BUYandHOLD gets your money, it buys the stock you've selected. BUYandHOLD charges $2.99 per trade.

Both of these services will buy you whatever portion of one share (or multiple of shares) you can afford with the dollar amount you choose to invest. If you invest $20 and choose a stock that sells for $10 a share, you'll get nearly two shares (minus a fraction for trading fees). If you choose a stock that sells for $60, you'll get roughly one-third of a share. As the months progress and you invest $20 again and again, you'll accumulate full shares in the companies of your choice.

Investors can set up accounts for either program online by going to the brokerage's Web pages and filling out a form.

Here are some of your other choices:

Mutual Funds

A HANDFUL OF big, well-respected mutual fund companies waive their normal investment minimums for people who agree to invest relatively small amounts regularly. While the typical fund company requires at least $50 per month, a few—at least as of late 1999—would take even less.

TIAA-CREF (800-223-1200) is a highly regarded fund company that is the biggest name in retirement savings for teachers. The company, which recently opened up to serve nonteachers as well, now offers funds in a variety of categories—growth, international, bond, and money market, for example—in which the company accepts regular deposits of as little as $25 per month. All the funds are highly rated. Additionally, by investing through a mutual fund, you get the benefit of wide diversification from your first $25 investment.

To find out about other low-minimum plans, go to **www.**

mfea.com and click on "Lowest Minimums." That provides you with an up-to-date listing of more than a dozen funds with standard minimum investment amounts of $500 or less. If you click on any specific fund, the site gives you details about that choice, such as the name of the fund manager, fees and performance, and whether the fund's standard minimum is waived for those who invest regularly.

Dividend Reinvestment Plans and Direct Stock Purchase Plans

ROUGHLY 1,000 COMPANIES nationwide offer investors the ability to buy their shares directly from the company. By and large, you must have one share of the company's stock registered in your name to start. After that, you can buy additional shares directly from the company either at no cost or at a very low cost.

The downside to most of these plans is speed. Normally share purchases are done just once a week or once a month (depending on the plan), so you can't time your buy or sell to correspond with some news event that's had a big impact on the stock price.

In addition, while most plans allow you to buy shares either very cheaply—for about $.03 per share or even for free—they often charge substantially more when you want to sell. It's not uncommon for companies to charge $.10 to $.12 per share on sales, for example. In other words, while it would cost you about $30 to buy 1,000 shares of stock, it could cost you $120 to sell those same 1,000 shares. Then, too, many of the companies that investors are most interested in buying—such as Microsoft, Qualcomm, Oracle, and Yahoo!, for example—don't offer direct stock purchase plans.

On the bright side, if a company you're interested in does offer such a plan, and you don't mind the processing delays, getting started is easy if you have Web access. Generally, you can go directly to the company's Web site and click on "investor relations," which tells you how to get started.

If you don't know whether a company offers a plan, or if you want to see just which companies do offer plans, there's no better place to go to find out than Netstock's Web page, at www.net-stock.com. This site lists hundreds of plans and often has direct links allowing you to sign up online.

Don't Delay

W HICHEVER PLAN YOU CHOOSE, REMEMBER JUST ONE THING: EVERY MOMENT YOU DELAY COSTS YOU MONEY. The most powerful word in all of finance is *compounding*. That means that the longer you leave your money invested, the more money you have in the long run.

Consider this little financial riddle: Who would have more money saved at retirement, the woman who socked away $2,000 a year for ten years—a total of $20,000—between the ages of twenty and thirty, or the man who saved twice as much for twice as long but didn't start until he was forty?

You guessed it: the woman. But how much more she would have might just surprise you. Because she left that $20,000 alone to compound for thirty-five additional years, until she turned age sixty-five, she landed a nest egg of $1,114,310. That's right—she would have more than $1.1 million.

Her male counterpart, who saved four times more of his own money—$80,000 total—would generate a nest egg worth just $416,465. (These figures assume that they both earned 10 percent on average on their money and they both retired at age sixty-five.) In other words, if you start early, it's easy to save even vast amounts. Wait, and the work becomes increasingly harder.

The moral of this story is that it doesn't matter how little you've got. Get started now and make your money grow.

chapter 13

How to Fix Your Broken Records

B ARBARA KNOWS EXACTLY how much she paid for 100 shares of stock way back in 1962. It's what's happened since then that makes her fuzzy. That's because she's been reinvesting dividends for the past twenty-six years. She never stopped to calculate how much extra money that amounted to. But now that she's considering selling the stock, she's in a quandary.

Going through twenty-six years of records to tabulate her total investment, including reinvested dividends, will be a horrible—maybe even impossible—job. But if she doesn't do it, she may pay too much in tax.

Her story is by no means unique. Investment professionals maintain that record keeping is one of the most important and most widely ignored steps in wise investing. Good records help you monitor your portfolio and help you determine when to buy and sell. They're also pivotal when you're determining how much tax you have to pay. And they can signal whether something is wrong with the way your broker or other financial advisers are handling your accounts.

"We try to explain to people that record keeping is the financial equivalent of getting an annual physical," says Richard A. Armellini, vice president and branch manager at Fidelity Investments in Los Angeles. "It helps you keep up with fees and performance, and it can save you a fortune if you [pay by the hour to] have your tax return professionally prepared."

Yet many investors fail to do it. If you've never set up an adequate system, the process is ponderous. But it doesn't need to be. If you start early and do it right, keeping good records will save you time and money.

Getting Organized

ELLEN NORRIS GRUBER, AUTHOR OF *THE PERSONAL FINANCE KIT* AND CO-OWNER OF A BURLINGAME, CALI-fornia, company called Go Get Organized, suggests that you buy a large three-ring binder, a three-hole punch, and some colored binder tabs. That will set you back $15 to $20, but these materials can serve as a basis for your investment records for decades, she says.

Next, divide the binder into sections for specific investments or types of accounts. Some people, particularly those with large, diverse portfolios that have actively traded investments, set their records up by date instead, keeping track of trades on a month-by-month basis. But an investment-by-investment approach works nicely if you have a manageable number of investments that you hold for long periods.

With taxable accounts, you should label each segment with the name of the investment—"XYZ Co." for instance, or "XYZ Mutual Fund." If you have tax-favored retirement accounts, such as 401(k)s, IRAs, or Keoghs, you may want to label them by the name of the account instead. You might have a section called "John's 401(k)" or "Mary's IRA," for example.

Why label the section with the IRA moniker rather than the investments held in it? Because one of the primary reasons that you keep these records is to determine your taxable gains and losses. Investments held through a retirement account all have the same tax properties. You can sell IBM at a profit and buy a new stock—or keep the profit in cash—and as long as the money stays in the IRA, there is no tax consequence. The only time you'll have to determine your tax bill when selling investments in a tax-deferred IRA, Keogh, or 401(k) is when you pull the money out of the account to spend it. Then the tax will be assessed on the entire amount—principal, interest, and capital gains.

With other investments, taxes are due in any year that you collect income or sell them at a profit. On the other hand, you can generate a capital loss if you sell when the stock price drops below your purchase price, which can offset other gains. You cannot deduct capital losses in tax-deferred accounts from capital gains or ordinary income.

The third step is to create a page that summarizes that particular investment. This summary should include how much you initially invested, your cost of investment—such as brokerage fees—and any subsequent investments you've made in that stock, bond, or mutual fund. The initial costs (including brokerage fees or mutual fund loads and sales commissions) as well as the amounts of subsequent investments will all determine your tax basis—the total cost of the investment—when it comes time to determine your taxable gain when you sell. Those who fail to keep track of the brokerage fees and reinvested dividends, or of the initial cost of the stock, may pay too much tax.

When you sell shares, the custodian or transfer agent will send both you and the IRS a 1099b showing the proceeds from the sale. Barring information to the contrary, the IRS assumes that the entire amount is profit. You must establish your cost by maintaining investment records. If you can't establish your cost basis in the investment, you could end up overtaxed.

After you've got your system set up, all you need to do is file the periodic account statements behind the summary page for each investment. It's wise to briefly review each statement when it comes in to make sure there are no errors or other discrepancies.

Once a year, you should update your summary page to indicate additional investments or sales and taxable profits. The summary page serves as a quick reference guide for you or your tax accountant when you want to determine your tax obligation for the year. It should also give you a good idea of how your individual investments and your portfolio as a whole are faring.

Can you delete a section when you sell an investment? Not immediately. You should save those records for at least four years, just in case you're audited by federal or state tax authorities.

What if you're in Barbara's situation—you've been investing for years without keeping good records and are now uncertain about where you stand?

You could estimate and hope you aren't audited, of course. If you are going to do it right, though, ask your broker, mutual fund company, or investment adviser to help you reconstruct your account history. In some cases, you'll be charged a fee for copies of old account statements or for the adviser's time. If the account isn't terribly old, the fees are likely to be modest, and the job will be manageable. But the longer you wait, the more difficult it becomes.

Keeping Tabs on Your Investments

I F YOU START EARLY AND DO IT REGULARLY, KEEPING
GOOD INVESTMENT RECORDS IS A SNAP. HERE'S A SAM-
ple worksheet. You would use one for each security you own in a
taxable account.

WORKSHEET

Investment Record

Investment _____

Per-share purchase price	$_____
Date purchased	_____ / _____ / _____
Number of shares	_____
Total initial investment	$_____
Brokerage/trading fees	$_____
Total invested, initial year	$_____

Subsequent investment _____

Year	_____
Additional amount invested	$_____
Shares acquired/new total	_____ / _____
Reinvested dividends	_____
Brokerage/trading fees	_____
Total invested to date	$_____

Subsequent investment _____

Year	_____

Additional amount invested $_____

Shares acquired/new total   _____/_____

Reinvested dividends   _____

Brokerage/trading fees   _____

Total invested to date $_____

Subsequent investment _____

Year   _____

Additional amount invested $_____

Shares acquired/new total   _____/_____

Reinvested dividends   _____

Brokerage/trading fees   _____

Total invested to date $_____

Subsequent investment _____

Year   _____

Additional amount invested $_____

Shares acquired/new total   _____/_____

Reinvested dividends   _____

Brokerage/trading fees   _____

Total invested to date $_____

chapter 14

Getting Help

OK. You've read the book. You know that you probably can invest on your own. But what if you don't want to? What if you prefer to hire someone to help you allocate your assets, pick individual stocks, and occasionally just hold your hand when the market activity makes you nervous?

Then you need to hire a financial planner to help. However, choose your planner carefully. Get recommendations. Look for important professional designations. And check out the planner with state and federal securities regulators to make sure he or she doesn't have a criminal record or a history pockmarked with investor complaints. After all, your future comfort may hinge on just how well this planner serves your best interests.

Choosing Among Financial Planners

BEFORE YOU START LOOKING, IT IS ALSO IMPORTANT TO KNOW HOW FINANCIAL PLANNERS EARN THEIR MONEY. There are three different options: commissions, fees, or a combination of both.

Commission-based planners are usually paid out of what you invest. For example, if you invest $10,000 in a mutual fund with a 5 percent load, only $9,500 is actually invested. The other $500 is paid to the planner who recommended this fund to you. Commission-based planners also make money from commissions generated from selling you life and disability insurance, limited partnerships, and other investments.

Unfortunately, many consumers are drawn to commission-based planners simply because it appears that their advice is free. That's because the commissions paid on many of these products are hidden or subtle. You don't see the commission that's paid on a whole life insurance policy when you purchase it, but it will certainly affect your long-term return. In fact, the commission on a whole life policy often amounts to 100 percent of your first-year premium. If a planner sells you a limited partnership or a viatical settlement, a big portion of what you've paid has also been eaten up in commissions paid to the planner that are largely invisible to you. By the same token, you may not pay a lot of attention to them, but the loads and 12b-1 fees charged by mutual funds can also dramatically reduce your long-term returns.

If, on the other hand, you go to a **fee-only planner**, you will pay to have a plan drawn up for you. For a comprehensive plan, it's not unusual to be charged between $1,000 and $2,000 for the service. However, a fee-only planner has no financial incentive to steer you toward a product that pays the planner better than it pays you.

Meanwhile, a planner who is paid through **both fees and commissions** usually charges less up front but will recommend some products that will pay the planner a commission. A planner in this category may recommend no-load funds, for example, but get commissions for selling you life and disability insurance. Commissions are typically computed as a percentage of what you spend.

It has become popular to say that you should never hire a commission based planner. That's simply because a planner who charges by commission may sometimes be tempted to sell you a product that's less attractive for you but pays the planner a fat commission. After all, even planners have to eat. Instead, many financial journalists steer their readers solely to fee-only planners because of the apparent conflicts of interest with commission-based planners.

This is easy but not always helpful advice. There are many good commission-based planners who have been in business for decades because they offer good advice that isn't influenced by whether or not they're earning a commission. Moreover, although you must realize that commission-based advice is not free, this payment system may simply work better for some families.

Plopping down $2,000 to pay a planner up front may leave you with nothing left to invest, for instance. So it may make more sense for you to invest the $2,000, knowing that a portion of that amount and of your subsequent investments will pay the planner. Yes, that may cost you more over time than simply paying up front. But you'll also have gotten started, which you might not have done if you had used up all your money buying advice.

If you do seek advice from a commission-based planner, you should make sure that you are sophisticated enough to evaluate whether the promise of a commission is affecting your planner's advice. If you find your planner is constantly pushing insurance, high-load funds, limited partnerships, or other unfamiliar investments, you should start asking questions.

On the insurance side, you need to consider just how much insurance you need and compare that to the amount your planner wants to sell. You should also know that term insurance is almost always a better deal than whole life insurance, particularly if you have a young family that needs lots of financial protection. But whole life insurance pays far higher commissions to the planner. If insurance is a big-ticket item for your family, check out a series titled "Insurance 101" that is posted on the *Los Angeles Times* Web page, at www.latimes.com/insure101. If your planner is pressing you to buy more insurance than you think you need, ask how he or she arrived at that number. Your planner may have thought about some valid expense that didn't occur to you or may simply not understand your family as well as you do. If you can't come to a meeting of the minds, look for another planner.

If your planner is recommending high-load funds, ask him or her to explain precisely why this fund is better than similar low-load or no-load funds. Expect data, including year-by-year returns, background on the fund manager, and Morningstar rankings on how the rest of the fund's peer group has performed. If your planner cannot give you this information, view the advice skeptically.

If your planner is recommending limited partnerships or viatical settlements, think very seriously about finding another planner. These are not investments that are well suited to beginning investors. And some might argue that these investments are not well suited to anyone. Yet they pay hefty commissions to people who sell them.

The ADV Form

HOW DO YOU KNOW how your planner is paid? Ask.

Registered financial advisers are required to fill out an extensive form called an ADV-Advisers form. The planner must file this form with securities regulators, and regulators expect planners to make at least the second part of it available to their clients. The ADV, Part II, discusses how the planner is paid, the type of business he or she specializes in, and other facts about the financial planning firm. However, the first part of the ADV form includes the planner's disciplinary history—little tidbits of information like whether the planner has ever been fined or suspended for absconding with customer money or making inappropriate investment recommendations to clients. Obviously, this is information you ought to know before you hire.

Ask for this form—both Part I and Part II. Read it. Make sure you understand the pertinent sections before you entrust your financial life to a planner. If the planner doesn't want to give you the first part of the form, consider it a warning sign. Then call the National Association of Securities Dealers (NASD) public disclosure hotline (800-289-9999). They should have a record of your planner's disciplinary history. (You can—and should—call the NASD line if you want to check the disciplinary history of a stockbroker, too.)

Professional Designations

WHEN INTERVIEWING PLANNERS, you should also look for their professional designations, which are often listed in an alphabetical jumble after their names on their business cards. There are literally dozens of professional designations that planners can and do trot out—CFP, ChFC, CLU, CPA, EA, CFS, CMFC, and PFS, to name a few. Some of these designations are important—a sign that your planner has more education and skill than the average Joe. Some, though, are insignificant. And some designations are simply made up.

Which are the important designations?

❑ **CFP** stands for **Certified Financial Planner.** This designation means that the planner has taken an extensive education course, passed exams, and has worked in the industry for at least three years. CFPs are also monitored by the Certified Financial Planner Board of Standards, which requires that they adhere to rules of ethical conduct and continue their education. If they don't, their designation is pulled. It is one of the first, and most important, professional designations you should look for when hiring a planner.

❑ **CPA** stands for **Certified Public Accountant**, which indicates your adviser has a financial background, has passed a grueling examination, and has at least two years of public accounting experience. A CPA who also has a **PFS** designation (for **Personal Financial Specialist**) has taken some extra training in personal financial planning. These designations are also policed by the American Institute of Certified Public Accountants, which requires CPAs to continue taking classes to keep their skills up-to-date.

❑ **CFA** stands for **Chartered Financial Analyst**—another prestigious designation that requires training, testing, and licensing. CFAs must undergo rigorous training in portfolio management, securities analysis, and economics, among other things. However, CFAs typically don't set up shop to deal with individual clients. They typically work for mutual fund companies, where they manage large portfolios for mutual funds and for other big institutions. However, if you're checking out a fund manager's credentials, this is one to look for.

❑ **CLU and ChFC** are designations given to people who have taken financial training concentrated on insurance issues.

❑ The National Association of Personal Financial Advisors, a trade group made up of fee-only planners, has created a special designation, **F-O (fee-only)**, to indicate that the planner doesn't take commissions. Don't attach too much significance to the absence of this designation, because you're going to find out how your planner is paid by reading his or her ADV form.

What about the ten zillion other acronyms? Some of them indicate that your adviser has taken a special class. Some of them indicate that he or she has passed a test. Some indicate that he or she specializes in some specific area, such as estate planning. (However, if you're wealthy enough to have to worry about estate planning—that would be if you had assets in excess of $675,000 as a single person, or $1.3 million as a married couple—you'll need to be concerned about other qualifications, such as law degrees, too. But that's a topic for another book.)

When confronted with an alphabet soup of unfamiliar professional designations, ask what they're all about. If somebody is touting these initials, they should certainly be able to explain why they're important. Make sure you know who gives the designation, what kind of training and/or experience is required to get it and keep it, and whether the designations are permanent or if they can be pulled if the planner breaches the group's rules or ethics. Obviously, designations that require continuing education and monitoring are more significant than ones that don't.

Finding a Planner

I F YOU WANT SOME HELP FINDING A PLANNER, THERE ARE SEVERAL GOOD RESOURCES AVAILABLE. THE FINAN cial Planning Association (800-282-PLAN) offers referrals to planners in your area. If you're looking for a fee-only planner, call the National Association of Personal Financial Advisors (888-FEE-ONLY). If you want a CPA with a Personal Financial Specialist designation, call the American Institute of Certified Public Accountants (888-777-7077 or visit their Web site at www.cpapfs.org). All of these organizations will happily provide you with lists of professionals in your area.

Hiring a Planner

WHEN YOU GET DOWN to the business of hiring a planner, figure it's going to take some time. You should get the names of at least three to five planners, check their professional designations and their disciplinary histories, and if those look good, go to interview them in person.

Realize that choosing a planner is a lot like choosing a doctor. Part of it is objective—the training and professional designations, for example. Part of it is subjective. Do you feel comfortable pouring out the details of your financial life to this person? Are you comfortable with the type of advice he or she is giving? Is the planner willing to explain things to you clearly and in detail, so that you know not only why he or she is making the recommendation but also how it fits into your life and your portfolio?

Planners should be willing to sit down with you and discuss what type of clients they normally work with; how they charge for their services; and what they charge for and what you get for free. (For instance, some fee-only planners charge by the hour; others will have you give them a retainer that allows you to call and ask advice numerous times throughout the year at no additional charge.)

They should be willing to show you plans they have done for others (with the other clients' names removed, of course) so you can get an idea of what kinds of recommendations they make and why.

During this interview process, you should be looking for a couple of things: Is the planner candid? Is there any area that he or she seems unwilling to discuss? Does he or she handle a lot of people like you? (It's helpful to deal with planners who specialize. For instance, if you're a teacher, it's good to deal with a planner who has many other teachers as clients, because he or she is likely to have more experience with the particular issues that affect your profession—such as 403(b) plans, which are likely to be your main source of retirement savings, and the "government pension offset" that can reduce or eliminate your Social Security benefits.)

Make sure the planners you're considering pass all the objective tests. But also subject them to your own inner voice—the one that normally tells you whether you trust someone. All too often, individuals get intimidated by financial professionals, so they ignore the uneasy feeling they have when dealing with them. They get talked into investments they don't understand because they assume the planner is smarter or more educated. Don't. Remember this and only this: This is your money. What happens to it will determine how well you and your family live in the future. Make sure that you feel very comfortable—both personally and professionally—with anyone who gives you financial advice.

Glossary

ADRs: American Depositary Receipts, which are securities traded on U.S. stock exchanges that represent shares in a foreign concern. Generally, these are similar to owning shares in a foreign company; however, they bear less currency risk (see Chapter 10).

ADV: A form that financial advisers are required to file by the Securities and Exchange Commission, which is the chief regulator in the securities industry. The form discloses a financial adviser's training, background, and employment arrangements, including whether the adviser has been disciplined by regulators and how the adviser is paid.

Call date: The point when the issuer of a bond can redeem (or pay off) outstanding bonds prior to the bond's maturity date.

Calls or call options: Securities that give the holder the right to buy a particular security at a set price by a specific date in the future.

Capital gain: A profit earned on a capital asset, such as stock or real estate. The term is also used to describe the favorable tax rate you pay when earning a profit on capital assets. (Whereas ordinary income is taxed at a 15 percent, 28 percent, 36 percent, or 39.6 percent federal rate, capital gains are taxed at either 10 percent or 20 percent, depending on your ordinary income tax bracket.)

Certificate of deposit: A contract with a bank whereby you agree to deposit a set amount for a set period of time. In turn, the bank agrees to pay you a set rate of interest. CDs, like other bank deposits, are insured by the federal government to $100,000 per depositor.

Closed-end funds: A type of mutual fund that offers just a fixed number of shares and trades on a major exchange, much like the stock of individual corporations (see Chapter 8).

CMOs: Collateralized Mortgage Obligations are a hybrid form of mortgage-backed securities aimed at defining and dividing the risk of mortgage securities among different investors (see Chapter 4).

Commodities: Bulk goods, such as food, coffee, grain, livestock, and metals, that are traded on the commodities exchange.

Corporate bonds: IOUs issued by individual corporations. When you buy a corporate bond, you are lending that company money in exchange for the promise that the company will pay you interest on your loan at regular intervals.

CPI: The Consumer Price Index is a cost-of-living benchmark aimed at measuring inflation in the United States. Published by the Bureau of Labor Statistics, the CPI determines cost-of-living adjustments on everything from Social Security benefits to tax schedules.

Currency risk: The chance that an investor in a foreign security will lose buying power during the conversion of stock sale proceeds from a foreign currency to U.S. dollars (see Chapter 10).

Default: When a company (or government entity) is unable to pay regularly scheduled principal or interest payments to bondholders.

Defined benefit plan: A type of pension that promises set monthly payments for the life of the pensioner (or the life of both the pensioner and his or her spouse).

Derivatives: A hybrid security that's formed by taking a traditional investment and turning it into a nontraditional security through the magic of investment banking. By and large, derivatives are designed to solve some specific problem or reduce some specific risk with the underlying investment. Unfortunately, with every risk that's eliminated, a new risk is created.

Dividend: Payments of cash or stock that represent a distribution of corporate earnings to shareholders.

Dividend yield: The annual percentage return earned by an investor from the payment of cash or stock through dividends. The dividend yield is calculated by comparing the market price of the stock to the annual per-share dividends. In other words, if a company pays $1 per share in dividends each year and the stock sells for $50 per share, that stock would have a 2 percent dividend yield.

DRIPS: Really geeky people or Dividend Reinvestment Plans, depending on the context. Dividend Reinvestment Plans automatically reinvest shareholder dividends at set intervals, providing the investor with additional shares in the company's stock.

Earnings per share: The amount of earnings allocated to each share of a company's outstanding stock. (A company with 1 million shares outstanding and $1.2 million in profits would report $1.20 in per-share earnings.)

Exchange rate: The price at which one country's currency can be converted into another country's currency. (In other words, you might get 100 Japanese yen for each U.S. dollar.)

Fannie Mae and Freddie Mac: Quasi-governmental entities that buy mortgages from lenders, consolidate them into pools of loans with like interest rates and maturity dates, and then resell them to investors. Technically, Fannie Mae is short for the Federal National Mortgage Association, while Freddie Mac is the nickname for the Federal Home Loan Mortgage Corporation.

Ginnie Mae: The cute name for the Government National Mortgage Association, which functions much like Fannie Mae and Freddie Mac.

Inflation: The rise in the cost of goods and services.

Initial public offering (IPO): The first offering of a company's stock to the general public.

IRAs: Individual Retirement Accounts are personal, tax-deferred retirement accounts that allow qualifying individuals to set aside up to $2,000 per year in retirement savings and deduct that amount from their income in the current tax year.

Money market account: A bank account that pays somewhat higher interest than a savings account but imposes certain restrictions on depositors, such as a requirement to maintain a high minimum balance.

Money market mutual fund: An open-ended mutual fund that invests in relatively safe, short-term investments such as short-term commercial paper, bank deposits, and Treasury bills.

Municipal bonds (munis): IOUs issued by state and local governments. Generally, these bonds pay relatively low rates of return, but the interest paid is free from both federal and state income taxes.

P/E: Price/earnings ratio is a method of measuring a company's market price relative to its earnings (see Chapter 5). It's calculated by dividing a company's current market price by its annual earnings per share. A company that sells for $50 per share and earns $2 per share would have a P/E of 25.

Portfolio: The combined investment holdings of an individual, which may include stocks, bonds, real estate, cash, and other investments.

Put: A security that grants the holder the right to sell shares of a specific stock at a set price by a certain date in the future. Someone owning a $35 put on XYZ Co., for example, can sell that stock for $35 on or before the expiration date, even if XYZ's market price declines to $30.

Real-return bonds: A type of bond that is aimed at keeping direct pace with the U.S. inflation rate (see Chapter 4).

REITs: Real Estate Investment Trusts are companies, which are often publicly traded, that manage portfolios of rental properties, passing on to investors the profits from both real estate sales and rents.

Share: A unit of equity ownership in either a corporation or a mutual fund.

Tax basis: The cost, for tax purposes, of a capital asset, such as a stock or real estate. In other words, what you paid for your holdings in a particular stock, inclusive of commissions and fees. This gets deducted from the sales price to determine your taxable profit when you sell the asset.

Trading volume: The number of shares of stock that are traded during a given period, usually one day.

Treasury bills: Short-term government debt issued to investors. Treasury bills mature (pay back principal to investors) in one year or less.

Treasury bonds: Long-term government debt, which takes more than ten years to mature.

Treasury notes: Medium-term government debt, with maturities ranging from two to ten years.

Viatical settlements: Life insurance policies sold by old or ailing policyholders for a fraction of the death benefit (see Chapter 4).

Index

About Bloomberg

BLOOMBERG L.P., founded in 1981, is a global information services, news, and media company. Headquartered in New York, the company has nine sales offices, two data centers, and 85 news bureaus worldwide.

Bloomberg, serving customers in 126 countries around the world, holds a unique position within the financial services industry by providing an unparalleled range of features in a single package known as the BLOOMBERG PROFESSIONAL™ service. By addressing the demand for investment performance and efficiency through an exceptional combination of information, analytic, electronic trading, and Straight Through Processing tools, Bloomberg has built a worldwide customer base of corporations, issuers, financial intermediaries, and institutional investors.

BLOOMBERG NEWS℠, founded in 1990, provides stories and columns on business, general news, politics, and sports to leading newspapers and magazines throughout the world. BLOOMBERG TELEVISION®, a 24-hour business and financial news network, is produced and distributed globally in seven different languages. BLOOMBERG RADIO™ is an international radio network anchored by flagship station BLOOMBERG® WBBR 1130AM in New York.

In addition to the BLOOMBERG PRESS® line of books, Bloomberg publishes *BLOOMBERG® MARKETS, BLOOMBERG PERSONAL FINANCE™*, and *BLOOMBERG® WEALTH MANAGER*. To learn more about Bloomberg, call a sales representative at:

Frankfurt:	49-69-92041-200	São Paulo:	5511-3048-4500
Hong Kong:	85-2-2977-6600	Singapore:	65-212-1200
London:	44-20-7330-7500	Sydney:	61-2-9777-8601
New York:	1-212-318-2200	Tokyo:	81-3-3201-8950
San Francisco:	1-415-912-2980		

FOR IN-DEPTH MARKET INFORMATION and news, visit the Bloomberg website at **www.bloomberg.com,** which draws from the news and power of the BLOOMBERG PROFESSIONAL™ service and Bloomberg's host of media products to provide high-quality news and information in multiple languages on stocks, bonds, currencies, and commodities.

About the Author

LOS ANGELES TIMES business writer **Kathy Kristof** is nationally known for her twice-weekly syndicated personal finance column, which reaches 40 million readers in more than 50 major newspapers (she replaced the late Sylvia Porter in bylining this highly visible column in 1991). Esteemed by her journalist peers (cited as "maybe the best reporter of all the personal finance columnists" in the prestigious TJFR 1999 Blue Chip Newsroom ranking of the top 100 American business journalists), she has received numerous writing awards and honors, including the title of 1998 Consumer Advocate of the Year by the California Alliance for Consumer Education. She is a sought-after lecturer at investment conferences and appears regularly on radio and television news programs. Kathy lives in southern California with her husband and their two children.